Best of Sahir

Best of Sahir

Kuldip Salil

rajpal

₹ 395
ISBN : 9789350643112
1st Edition : 2016, 7th Reprint : 2025

BEST OF SAHIR LUDHIANVI (Poetry)
(English translation of selected Urdu poetry of Sahir Ludhianvi)
Selected and translated by Kuldip Salil
Printed at G.S. Offeset, Delhi

RAJPAL & SONS
1590, Madarsa Road, Kashmere Gate, Delhi-110006
Phone : 011-23869812, 23867791
e-mail : sales@rajpalpublishing.com
www.rajpalpublishing.com
www.facebook.com/rajpalandsons

To
My brother Mulk Raj,
who is a contemporary of
Sahir Ludhianvi

INTRODUCTION

Founded in 1936, the Progressive Writers Association (PWA) has attracted perhaps the largest number of prominent Urdu writers. The list includes such leading lights as Ali Sardar Jafri, Faiz Ahmed Faiz, Mujaz Lukhnavi, Sajjad Zahir and many more. The PWA was in fact a movement against social inequalities, injustice, oppression and exploitation, and as such had widespread appeal not only among the Urdu poets, fiction writers and critics but also among writers and thinkers across the spectrum. By temperament, experience and training Sahir belongs to this movement.

Sahir Ludhianvi, whose full name was Abdul Hai Sahir Ludhianvi, was born in 1921 in Ludhiana, Punjab. His father, Fazal Mohammad lived a luxurious life much beyond his means. Sahir's mother, who was one of Fazal Mohammand's 11 wives, got fed up with her husband's outlandish living and after a period of strained relations got divorced from him. Sahir felt revolted by his father's behavior and in the court expressed his preference to remain with his mother. The father was so infuriated that notwithstanding the fact that Sahir was his only son or perhaps the only child, disinherited him from his landed property. He also declared that he would not let Sahir live with his mother even if he had to get him killed. Not only was a life of luxury lost to Sahir, he was compelled to live a life of poverty and extreme hardship. So much so that his mother had to sell her ornaments and Sahir had to take up most disagreeable sundry jobs to make both ends meet. In view of the threat from his father, his mother had to take special care of him.

Because of his father's behaviour and his mother's loving care, Sahir developed a feeling of hatred not only against his father but against all men who loved a loose life of lechery and luxury. At the same time, he developed feeling of tremendous sympathy for the unfortunate women like his mother. In poem after poem and in so many film songs that he wrote, this sympathy oozes out :

औरत ने जन्म दिया मर्दों को, मर्दों ने उसे बाज़ार दिया–

(Woman gave birth to man and man returned the favour by putting her up in the market-place.)

Some of Sahir's most soulful poems on prostitutes and other persecuted women have also to be understood in terms of his personal experience. Out of a life of great hardship with his mother and a conflict sometimes even between life and death was born Sahir, the poet. All his sorrows, bitterness, sympathies and aversions gushed forth from his heart in the form of verses.

After partition, Sahir spent a year in Delhi. Here he worked as a co-editor for the Urdu journal 'Shahrah'. He would wake up not before 10 AM, sit lazily in his bed as if contemplating for a long while and then start his day's work. Sahir greatly enjoyed the company of friends, reciting his own poems and those of others alongwith interesting anecdotes. Like most poets, he too sought and greatly relished his audience's approval and applause. I distinctly remember an afternoon in the year 1964 when some of us spotted him in Delhi University library. We requested him to recite some poems. He not only readily agreed (even though we were only five or six of us) but every time he read a couplet or a full poem, he would also ask how we liked it. A keen desire for praise or approval was easily discernible. Sahir had a phenomenal memory and could rattle off full text of letters and criticism on his poems published in various literary journals. He would ply his friends with cigarettes and endless cups of tea. These gatherings would go on till midnight. Then he would lapse into loneliness. Next morning, however, he would once again meet his friends enthusiastically.

When Sahir started writing poetry, Faiz, Firaq and Majaz were ruling the roost. No progressive poet, in fact no new poet remained uninfluenced by them. Sahir too came under their sway, especially that of Faiz Ahmed Faiz. However the tone, tenor and temperament of his poetry soon began to be determined by his own experience—the cruelty and arrogance of his father, the girl he loved and the heartbreaks he suffered and the poverty, trials and travails he had gone through in life. Then there was the influence of progressive writers' movement. His poetry has a strong social message. Sahir was against all social institutions that tolerate inequality, exploitation and discrimination. He was a friend of the poor and the oppressed. He was a rebel. After matriculation, he joined Government College, Ludhiana, but was expelled from there for his participation in the activities of All India Students' Federation, affiliated to the Communist Party of India. After that he joined Government College, Lahore but was expelled from there also for the same reason. In Lahore, he edited 'Adab-e-Latif' and 'Savera'. He then came to Delhi and from there moved to Bombay to live there permanently. That he wrote poetry from his own experience is evident from such lines as :

मैं उन अजदाद का बेटा हूं जिन्होंने पैहम
अजनबी क़ौम के साये की हिमायत की है
ग़दर के सायाने-नापाक से लेकर अब तक
हर कड़े वक़्त में सरकार की ख़िदमत की है—

(I am a descendant of those ancestors
Who have always favoured the foreign rule
Starting with the failed mutiny to the present day
They have stood by the government on every occasion)

And then;

न कोई जादा, न मंज़िल न रोशनी न सुराग़
भटक रही है ख़लाओं में ज़िंदगी मेरी
इन्हीं ख़लाओं में रह जाऊंगा कहीं खोकर
मैं जानता हूं मगर फिर भी—

(I see no road, no destination, no light, no clue
My life is floating about in empty spaces
Wherein I can very well be lost
I know it, but still...)

It was because of this authentic personal experience that Sahir could carve out a distinct niche for himself among Urdu poets and win praise. He wrote out of this experience as it came, of course with artistic embellishment and editing.

The sorrows of love and of the heartlessness of society that we come across in his poetry are sorrows felt and not a mere hearsay.

Sahir is essentially a romantic poet. Intensity of love and his failure in love leave everything behind:

मेरे ख़्वाबों के झरोखों को सजाने वाली
मेरे ख़्वाबों में तेरा गुज़र है कि नहीं...
पूछकर अपनी निगाहों से बता दे मुझको,
मेरी रातों के मुक़द्दर में सहर है कि नहीं।

(You who have settled in my dreams and illuminated them
Will you ever make my dreams a reality
Ask your eyes and tell me, pray
Will the dawn ever come my way.)

In frustration he declares that now he will never sing the songs in which there is :

...उम्मीद की गहराई भी
मौत के क़दमों की आहट भी जीवन की अंगड़ाई भी
मुस्तक़बिल की किरणें भी थीं हाल की बोझिल ज़ुल्मत भी
तूफ़ानों का शोर भी था ख़्वाबों की शहनाई भी!

(...the light of hope
The sound of the footsteps of death as well as life pulsating
The rays of future and heavy darkness of the present
The roar of storms as well as the sound of shehnai in my dreams...)

But he continues to write :

मेरी दरमांदा जवानी की तमन्नाओं के
मुज़महिल ख़्वाब की तदबीर बता दे मुझको

तेरे दामन में गुलिस्तां भी हैं वीराने भी
मेरा हासिल मेरी तक़दीर बता दे मुझको

(Tell me the fate of the yearnings
Of my faint and feeble youth
You can bestow a blooming garden as also yawning wilderness
Tell me pray which one is in store for me)

All his life Sahir kept asking such questions. And when he got no satisfactory answer, when these questions led to more troubling questions, he not only felt sad and gloomy, but was forced to think why true love was not requited. This led to a habit of contemplation where personal love transcends Sahir the individual and turns into love for all mankind. He starts with :

तुझको ख़बर नहीं मगर इक सादा-लोह को
बरबाद कर दिया दो दिन के प्यार ने...

(You may not know but a simple-hearted man
Stands ruined by your fickle love.)

He goes on to :

मैं और तुमसे तर्के-मुहब्बत की आरज़ू
दीवाना कर दिया ग़में-रोज़गार ने

(O never imagine that I would stop loving you
But ah, I have been driven crazy by the struggle for livelihood.)

And then bluntly declares :

तुम्हारे ग़म के सिवा और भी तो ग़म हैं मुझे
निज़ात जिनसे में इक लम्हा पा नहीं सकता
ये ऊंचे-ऊंचे मकानों की हवेलियों के तले
हर एक गाम पे भूखे भिखारियों की सदा
ये कारख़ाने में लोहे का शोरो-गुल जिसमें

है दफ़न लाखों गरीबों की रूह का नग़मा
गली-गली में ये बिकते हुए जवां चेहरे
हसीन आंखों में अफ़सुर्दगी-सी छाई हुई ये मेरे देश के लोग।

ये ग़म बहुत है मेरी ज़िंदगी मिटाने को
उदास रहके और दिल को रंज न दे—
तुम्हारे ग़म के सिवा और भी ग़म हैं मुझे

(Apart from sorrowing for you
I have other sorrows too
From which even for a moment there is no relief
In the backdrop of tall mansions, here
I hear the starving beggars calling.
Hunger and poverty stalking everywhere
I hear the hammer falling and beating
Iron into shape in the factories everywhere
These youthful maidens on sale
These lovely eyes filled with despair
These sorrows are enough to finish my life)
Do not make my life more miserable by remaining sad
There are other sorrows too
Apart from sorrowing for you

These sufferings in love and life, the sufferings which he underwent himself and the sufferings of the vast humanity at large—these sufferings instead of breaking his spirit, instead of leaving him depressed, imparted to him remarkable grit and determination not only to bear and overcome them but also to turn them into a source of pride and joy, besides inspiring him and becoming a source of some good poetry. This led him to try and comprehend the problems that confront not only him but also the times in which he lived. This gave birth to love and sympathy for less fortunate masses:

आज के मज़दूर, किसानों मेरे राग तुम्हारे हैं
फ़ाक़ाकश इनसानों मेरे गीत तुम्हारे हैं!

(From today, O the workers and peasants my songs are for you
O the hungry masses, to you my songs are dedicated.)

And here is Sahir the revolutionary :

आज से मेरे फ़न का मतलब ज़ंजीरें पिघलाना है
आज से मैं शबनम के बदले अंगारे बरसाऊंगा।

(From today, my art (poetry) will be used for melting the chains
From today instead of dew drops I will rain fire and fury.)

However, along with his poetry of revolt against the establishment, Sahir continued to write poetry of love; he continued to write traditional ghazals.

According to Sardar Jafri, Sahir was a split personality; he himself was responsible for anarchy in his personal life. One is reminded of a similar attack by Sardar Jafri on so great a poet as Faiz Ahmed Faiz. Great or not so great, split or sound, Sahir was first and last a poet, and a conscious one at that. Many an Urdu poet who were lured by the film industry, became less of a poet and more a famous man. Majrooh Sultanpuri is a case in point. In the present day to an extent, this is true of Javed Akhtar. But Sahir never lowered his level or compromised on poetry even in the film songs. In fact many of his masterpieces found place in films:

वो सुबह कभी तो आयेगी, वो सुबह कभी तो आयेगी
इन काली सदियों के सर से जब रात का आंचल ढलकेगा
जब दुख के बादल पिघलेंगे जब सुख का सागर छलकेगा,
जब अम्बर झूम के नाचेगा, जब धरती नग्मे गायेगी –
वो सुबह कभी तो आयेगी।
जिस सुबह की ख़ातिर जुग-जुग से हम सब मर-मरकर जीते हैं
जिस सुबह की अमृत की धुन में हम ज़हर के प्याले पीते हैं
इन भूखी-प्यासी रूहों पर इक दिन तो करम फ़रमायेगी
वो सुबह कभी तो आयेगी।

(Sooner or later that day will dawn, that day will dawn
When the veil of night will lift from over the head of dark centuries
When our sufferings will move away like the clouds and the ocean of joy overflow
When the sky and the earth will break into song and dance
Sooner or later that day will dawn
The dawn for which we have been living a life of death
The dawn to drink the nectre of which we gladly drink poison.
That dawn will surely oblige our thirsting and hungering spirit sooner or later.
Sooner or later that day will dawn.)

Or the famous:

चलो इक बार फिर से अजनबी बन जायें हम दोनों–
(Let us agree to become strangers again)

Sahir had the unique distinction of raising the film songs to the level of high poetry. When I say unique distinction I assert that neither Kaifi Azmi, nor Majrooh Sultanpuri nor Hasrat Jaipuri—in fact nobody was so conscious, so uniformally good as Sahir was. And then the range and variety of Sahir's songs is astonishing. He wrote not just the serious songs of love and human sufferings and of hope, his pen produced humorous and side splittingly funny witty ditties too. On being asked to write a song to fit the tune, he quipped, it is like preparing a coffin without seeing the dead body (कफ़न पहले और मुर्दा बाद में).

Then he wrote beautiful songs about children :

बच्चे मन के सच्चे...
इनको किसी से बैर नहीं इनके लिये कोई ग़ैर नहीं...

(The children are pure at heart...
They know no foe, nobody to them is a stranger.)

These songs are remarkable for their spontaneity and simplicity. This simplicity remains intact even when he writes socially significant, philosophical songs:

आगे भी जाने न तू, पीछे भी जाने न तू, जो भी है,
बस यही पल है...

(You know neither the future, nor have any control over you past, only the present moment is the thing for you.)

Sahir had a big ego, some would say, a bloated ego. He would insist that he should be paid one rupee more than the music director. And he turned down an award for a song he wrote for the film `Gumrah' saying, "Is it the only good song that I have written?" It is said that. even in sixties and seventies, he would not charge less than twenty-five thousand for his songs for a film. And then, he was extremely moody, even eccentric.

Like many Urdu poets, he was given to heavy drinking. His mother requested all his friends to make him give up or at least reduce his drinking. But Sahir would not listen. And on 20th October, 1980 he passed away at the age of fifty-nine.

Even when he was active in students' movement, Sahir was seriously devoting himself to poetry, and soon made his place among Urdu poets. His poetry, not just his lyrics but also the *nazms* are soul stirring. He was a progressive poet of great conviction and sincerity. Some of his verses like :

एक शहनशाह ने दौलत का सहारा लेकर
हम ग़रीबों की मुहब्बत का उड़ाया है मज़ाक़

(An emperor on the strength of his wealth and riches
Has made fun of poor lovers like us)

have become classic.

Sahir was a good poet, but was he a great poet? Perhaps not. He was very good in certain individual pieces but once you sit down with his collection, the impression changes. One finds him repetitive, even monotonous. Like Sahir, Faiz Ahmed Faiz was also a progressive poet, but his every poem has freshness about it. There is no harm if the poet is inspired by single idea and writes around that idea only. He can still be a great poet. Iqbal in Urdu and William Wordsworth in English are good examples of this. While Wordsworth wrote mostly about nature, Iqbal was possessed for the most part, by the idea of 'Khudi' (selfhood) and the upliftment of the oppressed, especially the oppressed Muslims of India and the world. The range of both Wordsworth and Iqbal may perhaps not be wide, but the depth of their poetry is great. This said, however, nothing can take away from Sahir's popularity as a good poet. And then his sincerity as a poet is beyond question:

आने वाली सदियां तुम को याद करेंगी हमउसरो
जब उनको ये पता चलेगा तुमने फ़िराक़ को देखा है

(The coming generations will revere you, my contemporaries
When they get to know that you have seen Firaq.)

This couplet by egotistical Firaq Gorakhpuri is at least partially true of Sahir Ludhianvi.

Kuldip Salil
1770 Outram Line
G.T.B. Nagar
Delhi-110009
Mob.: 9810052245
E-mail: poetkuldipsalil@gmail.com

Contents

Sahir Ludhianvi

चन्द कलियां नशात की[1] चुनकर
मुद्दतों महवे-यास रहता हूं
तेरा मिलना खुशी की बात सही
तुझसे मिलकर उदास रहता हूं

Chand kaliyan nashaat ki chunkar
Muddaton mahve-yaas rahata hun
Tera milana khushi ki baat sahi
Tujhse milkar udaas rahata hun

1. हर्ष की

I pick up some buds of happiness
And for long remain despair-clad
Meeting you is certainly a matter of joy
But after meeting you, I remain sad.

ताजमहल

ताज तेरे लिए इक मज़हरे-उल्फ़त[1] ही सही
तुमको इस वादी-ए-रंगीं[2] से अक़ीदत[3] ही सही

मेरी महबूब[4] कहीं और मिलाकर मुझसे:

बज़्मे-शाही[5] में ग़रीबों का गुज़र, क्या मानी?
सब्त[6] जिस राह पे हों सतवते-शाही[7] के निशां
उस पे उल्फ़त भरी रूहों का[8] सफ़र क्या मानी?

मेरी महबूब पसे-पर्दा-ए-तश्हीरे-वफ़ा[9]
तूने सतवत[10] के निशानों को तो देखा होता
मुर्दा शाहों के मक़ाबिर से[11] बहलने वाली!
अपने तारीक[12] मकानों को तो देखा होता।

→

Taj tere liye ek mazahare-ulfat hi sahi
Tumko is vadi-e-rangi se akidat hi sahi

Meri mahboob kahin aur milakar mujhse-!

Bazme-shahi mein garibon ka guzar, kya mani?
Sabt jis raah pe hon satvate-shahi ke nishan
Us pe ulfat bhari roohon ka safar kya mani?

Meri mahboob pase-parda-e-tashhire-wafa
Tune satwat ke nishano ko to dekha hota
Murda shahon ke makabir se bahlne wali!
Apne tarik makano ko to dekha hota.

---

1. प्रेम का द्योतक 2. रमणीय 3. श्रद्धा 4. प्रेयसी 5. शाही दरबार 6. अंकित 7. शाही वैभव के 8. आत्माओं का (प्रेमियों का) 9. वफ़ा के विज्ञापन के पर्दे के पीछे 10. वैभव 11. मक़बरों से 12. अंधकारपूर्ण

Taj Mahal

The Taj may be a symbol of love for you,
You may be fascinated by its view
But meet me somewhere else my beloved, my dear

In the courts of kings, the poor have no place
A place where pelf and power rule, how can the
loving souls find solace!

Behind this show of love you ought to have seen
my dear

These signs of grandeur stark
You, who are beguiled by the dead kings'
mausoleums
You ought to have remembered our houses dark

→

अनगिनत लोगों ने दुनिया में मोहब्बत की है
कौन कहता है कि सादिक़[1] न थे जज़्बे उनके
लेकिन उनके लिए तश्हीर[2] का सामान नहीं
क्योंकि वो लोग भी अपनी ही तरह मुफ़लिस[3] थे

ये इमारातो-मक़ाबिर[4] ये फ़सीलें, ये हिसार[5]
मुतलकुल्हुक्म[6] शहनशाहों की अज़मत[7] के सुतूं[8]
दामने-दहर[9] पे उस रंग की गुलकारी[10] है
जिसमें शामिल है तेरे और मेरे अज़दाद[11] का खूं[12]

मेरी महबूब! उन्हें भी तो मोहब्बत होगी
जिनकी सन्नाई ने[13] बख़्शी[14] है इसे शक्ले-जमील[15]
उनके प्यारों के मक़ाबिर रहे बेनामो-नमूद[16]
आज तक उन पे जलाई न किसी ने क़न्दील[17]

→

Anginat logon ne duniya mein mohabbat ki hai
Kaun kahata hai ki sadik na the jazbe unke
Lekin unke liye tashhir ka saman nahi
Kyonki vo log bhi apni hi tarah muflis the

Ye imarato-makabir ye fasilen, ye hisar
Mutlakulhukm shahanshahon ki azamat ke sutoo
Damne-dahar pe us rang ki gulalkari hai
Jisme shamil hai tere aur mere azadad ka khoon

Meri mahboob! unhe bhi to mohabbat hogi
Jinki sannai ne bakshi hai ise shakle-jamil
Unke pyaron ke makabir rahe benamo-namod
Aaj tak un pe jalai na kisi ne kandil

---

1. सच्चे 2. विज्ञापन 3. निर्धन 4. इमारतें और मक़बरे 5. क़िले 6. स्वेच्छाचारी 7. महानता 8. स्तम्भ 9. संसार के दामन पर 10. बेल-बूटे 11. पूर्वजों 12. लहू 13. कारीगरी ने 14. प्रदान की 15. सुन्दर रूप 16. जिनका कोई नाम व निशान तक नहीं 17. दीप

Numberless people have in this world loved
Who says their feelings were not true
But they could not advertise their lore
Because like us, they were poor too

These symbols of the aristocracy of kings and their imposing style
The palaces and mausoleums, these ramparts and the forts here

This glow on the face of the earth
Is because of the blood of our ancestors, my dear

They too must have loved my dear
Whose art has given it a form so fair
But the graves of their beloveds have remained obscure
And nobody has lit a candle there

→

ये चमनज़ार[1] ये जमना का किनारा, ये महल
ये मुनक़्क़श[2] दरो-दीवार, ये मेहराब, ये ताक़
इक शहनशाह ने दौलत का सहारा लेकर
हम ग़रीबों की मोहब्बत का, उड़ाया है मज़ाक

मेरी महबूब कहीं और मिलाकर मुझसे!

Ye chamanzar ye jamna ka kinara, ye mahal
Ye munakkash daro-diwar, ye mehraab, ye taak
Ek shahanshah ne daulat ka sahara lekar
Hum garibon ki mohabbat ka, udaya hai mazaak

Meri mehboob kahin aur milakar mujhse!

1. उद्यान 2. चित्रित

This garden here, this bank of river Yamuna, this
mansion palatial,
These engraved walls and ceilings, doors and minarets
with all the attendant fuss
An emperor on the strength of his wealth and riches
Has made fun of the poor lovers like us

Meet me somewhere else, my beloved dear!

तंग आ चुके हैं कश्मकशे-ज़िंदगी से हम
ठुकरा न दें जहां को कहीं बेदिली से हम

लो आज हमने तोड़ दिया रिश्ताए-उमीद[1]
लो अब कभी गिला न करेंगे किसी से हम

उभरेंगे एक बार अभी दिल के वलवले
गो दब गए हैं बारे-ग़मे-ज़िंदगी[2] से हम

गर ज़िंदगी में मिल गए फिर इत्तफाक़ से
पूछेंगे अपना हाल तेरी बेबसी से हम

अल्लाह रे फ़रेबे-मशीयत[3] कि आज तक
दुनिया के ज़ुल्म सहते रहे ख़ामुशी से हम

Tang aa chuke hain kashmkashe-zindagi se hum
Thukra na den jahan ko kahin bedili se hum

Lo aaj humne tod diya rishtaye-umeed
Lo ab kabhi gila na karenge kisi se hum

Ubharenge ek bar abhi dil ke valvale
Go dab gaye hain bare-game-zindgi se hum

Gar zindgi mein mil gaye phir ittafaak se
Puchhenge apna hal teri bebasi se hum

Allaha re farebe-mashiyat ki aaj tak
Duniya ke julm sahte rahe khaamushi se hum

---

1. उम्मीद से संबंध 2. जीवन की चिंताओं के बोझ से 3. दैव-इच्छा की प्रवंचना

The struggle and strains of life have driven me to the wall
I might kick the bucket in disgust, top bottom and all

From today, I will expect nothing from any one
From today, I will complain against none

My spirits will assert once again, I know
I am weighed down by the sorrows of life for now, though

If ever again we meet in life by any chance
I'll like to know my condition from your looks askance

What an irony, O God, what quirk of fate,
We're quietly suffering the cruelty of the world till this date

जब कभी उनकी तवज्जोह में कमी पाई गई
अज़-सरे-नौ दास्ताने-शौक़[1] *दुहराई गई*

बिक गए जब तेरे लब, फिर तुझको क्या शिकवा अगर
ज़िंदगानी वादा-ओ-साग़र से बहलाई गई

कैसे-कैसे चश्मो-आरिज़[2] *गर्दे-ग़म से बुझ गए*
कैसे-कैसे पैकरों की[3] *शाने-ज़ेबाई*[4] *गई*

दिल की धड़कन में तवाजुन[5] *आ चला है, ख़ैर हो*
मेरी नज़रें बुझ गईं या तेरी रानाई[6] *गई*

उनका ग़म, उनका तसव्वुर[7] *उनके शिकवे अब कहां?*
अब तो ये बातें भी ऐ दिल! हो गई आई-गई

Jab kabhi unki tavajjoh mein kami paai gai
Az-sare-nau dastane-shauk duhrai gai

Bik gaye jab tere lab, phir tujhko kya shikva agar
Zindgani wada-o-saagar se bahlaai gai

Kaise-kaise chashmo-aariz garde-gam se bujh gaye
Kaise-kaise paikaron ki shane-zebaai gai

Dil ki dharkan mein tawajun aa chala hai, khair ho
Meri nazaren bujh gai ya ranaai gai

Unka gam, unka tasavvur unke shikve ab kahan?
Ab to ye batein bhi ye dil! ho gai aai-gai

---

1. प्रेम-कथा 2. आंखें और कपोल 3. शरीरों की 4. सज्जा 5. संतुलन 6. लावण्यता 7. कल्पना

Whenever I find her attention wandering
I retell the story of our love from the beginning

Once you have sold out your love why should you mind
If in the goblet and the bottle some solace I find

What beauties have been reduced to dust by the sorrows of time
What shapes and forms have lost their lustre and prime!

God save us, some normalcy in my heartbeat I see
Am I going blind or, are you losing your charm and beauty?

Gone are my complaints against her, gone my suffering and my fancy high
These things too, O heart, are things of times gone by

परछाइयां

जवान रात के सीने पे दूधिया आंचल
मचल रहा है किसी ख़्वाबे-मरमरीं की[1] तरह
लचक रही हैं किसी जिस्मे-नाज़नीं की[2] तरह
फ़ज़ा में घुल से गए हैं उफ़ुक़ के[3] नर्म .ख़ुतूत[4]
ज़मीं हसीन है, ख़्वाबों की सरज़मीं की तरह

तसव्वुरात की[5] परछाइयां उभरती हैं
कभी गुमान[6] की सूरत कभी यक़ीं की तरह
वो पेड़ जिनके तले हम पनाह लेते थे
खड़े हैं आज भी साकित[7] किसी अमीं[8] की तरह

→

Jawan raat ke sine pe dudhiya aanchal
Machal raha hai kisi khwabe-marmarin ki tarah
Lachak rahi hain kisi jisme-nazanin ki tarah
Faza mein ghul se gaye hain ufuk ke narm khutut
Zamin hasin hai, khwabon ki sarzamin ki tarah

Tasavvuraat ki parchhaiyan ubharati hain
Kabhi gumaan ki surat kabhi yakin ki tarah
Vo ped jinke tale hum panaah lete the
Khade hain aaj bhi saakit kisi ameen ki tarah

1. मरमर-ऐसे (सुन्दर) सपने की 2. सुन्दरी के बदन की 3. क्षितिज के 4. रेखाएं 5. कल्पनाओं की 6. भ्रम 7. चुपचाप 8. साक्षी

Shadows

That milky spread over the bosom of the night so young
Naughty like a beautiful dream to you clung
Mesmerising flowers, bewitching leaves, beatific branches,
swinging alluringly like a beauty chic
The lines of the horizon have completely merged,
The earth is resplendent like the land of dreams.

The shadows of imagination well up!

Sometimes like a phantom and sometimes like a vision true
The trees that sheltered us
Stand till today, quietly, a witness through and through

→

इन्हीं के साये में फिर आज दो धड़कते दिल
ख़ामोश होंठों से कुछ कहने-सुनने आए हैं
न जाने कितनी कशाकश से[1], कितनी काविश से[2]
ये सोते जागते लम्हे चुराके लाए हैं

यही फ़ज़ा थी, यही रुत, यही ज़माना था
यहीं से हमने मोहब्बत की इब्तिदा[3] की थी
धड़कते दिल से, लरज़ती हुई निगाहों से
हुज़ूरे-ग़ैब में[4] नन्ही-सी इल्तिजा की थी

कि आरज़ू के कंवल खिल के फूल हो जाएं
दिलो-नज़र की दुआएं क़ुबूल हो जाएं

तसव्वुरात की परछाइयां उभरती हैं!

→

Inhi ke saye mein phir aaj do dharakte dil
Khamosh hoton se kuchh kahne-sunne aaye hain
Na jane kitni kashakash se, kitni kavish se
Ye sote jagate lamhe churake laye hain

Yahi faza thi, yahi rut, yahi zamana tha
Yahin se humne mohabbat ki ibtida ki thi
Dharakte dil se, larazati hui nigahon se
Huzure-gaib mein nanhi-si iltija ki thi

Ki aarzu ke kawal khil ke phool ho jayen
Dilo-nazar ki duayen kubool ho jayen

Tasavvuraat ki parchhaiyan ubharati hain!

---

1. यत्न से 2. प्रयत्न से 3. शुरुआत 4. भगवान की सेवा में

Today again under the bower two beating hearts
Have come to utter sweet nothings through the silent lips
No one knows with what effort and manoeuvre
These moments of sleep and wakefulness they have achieved

The same clime, the same seasons, the same age it was
The same point where our love began and blossomed
With panting heart, with quivering eyes
A request was made in the service of the divine
That the little buds of desire into flowers bloom
And the prayers of the heart find a befitting room

The shadows of imagination well up!

→

तुम आ रही हो ज़माने की आंख से बचकर
नज़र झुकाए हुए और बदन चुराए हुए
ख़ुद अपने क़दमों की आहट से झेंपती, डरती
ख़ुद अपने साए की जुंबिश से ख़ौफ़ खाए हुए

तसव्वुरात की परछाइयां उभरती हैं!

रवां है छोटी-सी कश्ती हवाओं के रुख़ पर
नदी के साज़ पे मल्लाह गीत गाता है
तुम्हारा जिस्म हर इक लहर के झकोले से
मेरी ख़ुली हुई बांहों में झूल जाता है

तसव्वुरात की परछाइयां उभरती हैं!

Tum aa rahi ho zamane ki aankh se bachkar
Nazar jhukaye huye aur badan churaye huye
Khud apne kadamon ki aahat se jhepti, darti
Khud apne saaye ki jumbish se khauf khaye huye

Tasavvuraat ki parchhaiyan ubharati hain!

Rawaan hai chhoti-si kashti hawaon ke rukh par
Nadi ke saaz pe mallah geet gata hai
Tumhara jism har ik lahar ke jhakole se
Meri khuli hui baahon mein jhool jata hai

Tasavvuraat ki parchhaiyan ubharati hain!

You are arriving stealthily, sneaking past the world
With your eyes downcast and your body coy
Fearful of the sounds of your own footsteps
In awe of the movement of your own shadow

The shadows of imagination well up!

The little boat floats, steered by the wind
The rhythm of the river stirs the boatman to sing
Your body with a rush of each wave
Swings into my open arms.

The shadows of imagination well up!

मादाम

आप बेवजह परेशान-सी क्यों हैं मादाम[1]
लोग कहते हैं तो फिर ठीक ही कहते होंगे
मेरे एहबाब ने[2] तहज़ीब न सीखी होगी
मेरे माहौल में[3] इन्सान न रहते होंगे

नूरे-सरमाया से[4] है रूए-तमद्दुन की[5] ज़िया[6]
हम जहां हैं वहां तहज़ीब नहीं पल सकती
मुफ़लिसी हिसे-लताफ़त को[7] मिटा देती है
भूख आदाब के[8] सांचे में नहीं ढल सकती

लोग कहते हैं तो लोगों प तअज्जुब़ कैसा
सच तो कहते हैं कि नादारों की[9] इ़ज्ज़त कैसी
लोग कहते हैं—मगर आप अभी तक चुप हैं
आप भी कहिए ग़रीबों में शराफ़त कैसी

→

Aap bewajah pareshan-si kyon hain maadaam
Log kahte hain to phir thik hi kahte honge
Mere ahbaab ne tahzeeb na sikhi hogi
Mere mahaul mein insaan na rahte honge

Noore-sarmaya se hai roohe-tamddun ki ziya
Hum jahan hain wahan tahzeeb nahin pal sakti
Muflisi hisse-lataafat ko mita deti hai
Bhookh aadab ke sanche mein nahin dhal sakti

Log kahte hain to logon pe tajjub kaisa
Sach to kahte hain ki nadaron ki izzat kaisi
Log kahte hain - magar aap abhi tak chup hain
Aap bhi kahiye gharibon mein sharafat kaisi

---

1. 'मैडम' का उर्दू रूपान्तर 2. मित्रों ने 3. वातावरण में 4. धन के प्रकाश से 5. सभ्यता के चेहरे की 6. चमक 7. कोमल भावना को 8. शिष्टता के 9. निर्धनों की

Madam

Don't be unnecessarily upset, madam
If people say it must be true
My clan must have remained uncivilized
And there must have been no human beings in my mileu

Of course, culture can flourish under the floodlights of capitalism
And not where we have our abode
Poverty indeed wipes out all delicate feelings
And a hungry person no manners knows.

It is not surprising that people say so,
It is true that the poor can no respect expect
People say so but you are quiet so far
You may also say that the poor lack all gentleness

→

नेक मादाम! बहुत जल्द वो दौर आएगा
जब हमें ज़ीस्त के अदवार[1] परखने होंगे
अपनी ज़िल्लत की क़सम, आपकी अज़मत[2] की क़सम
हमको ता'ज़ीम के[3] मेआर[4] परखने होंगे

हमने हर दौर में[5] तज़लील[6] सही है लेकिन
हमने हर दौर के चेहरे को ज़िया[7] बख़्शी है
हमने हर दौर में मेहनत के सितम झेले हैं
हमने हर दौर के हाथों को हिना[8] बख़्शी है

लेकिन इन तल्ख़ मुबाहिस से[9] भला क्या हासिल
लोग कहते हैं तो फिर ठीक ही कहते होंगे
मेरे एहबाब ने तहज़ीब न सीखी होगी
मैं जहां रहता हूं इन्सान न रहते होंगे

Nek maadaam! bahut jald vo daur aayega
Jab humein zist ke adwar parkhne honge
apni zillat ki kasam, aapki azmat ki kasam
humko ta'zeem ke meaar parkhne honge

Humne har daur mein tazleel sahi hai lekin
Humne har daur ke chehre ko ziya bakshi hai
Humne har daur mein mehnat ke sitam jhele hain
Humne har daur ke hathon ko hina bakhshi hai

Lekin in talkh mubahis se bhala kya hasil
Log kahte hain to phir thik hi kahte honge
Mere ahbab ne tahzeeb na sikhi hogi
Main jahan rahta hon insaan na rahte honge

---

1. जीवन के युग, मूल्य 2. महानता 3. आदर-सम्मान के 4. स्तर 5. काल में 6. अपमान 7. चमक-दमक 8. मेंहदी 9. कटु विवाद से

Noble madam, very soon the time will come
When the current values of life will have to be tested
I swear by our humiliation and your exaltedness
That the criteria of good manners will have to be re-examined

In every age we have faced humiliation
But it is we who have lent luster to every age
In every age our hard labour has been rewarded with atrocities
And it is we who have brightened the face of every age

But what is the use of these unseemly debates
If people say, it must be true.
My clan must have remained uncivilized
And there must have been no human beings in my mileu.

शिकस्त

अपने सीने से लगाए हुए उम्मीद की लाश
मुद्दतों ज़ीस्त को[1] नाशाद[2] किया है मैंने
तूने तो एक ही सदमे से किया था दो-चार
दिल को हर तरह से बर्बाद किया है मैंने
जब भी राहों में नज़र आए हरीरी-मलबूस[3]
सर्द आहों में तुझे याद किया है मैंने
और अब जबकि मेरी रूह की पहनाई में[4]
एक सुनसान-सी मग़मूम[5] घटा छाई है
तू दमकते हुए आरिज़ की[6] शुआएं[7] लेकर
गुलशुदा[8] शम्एं जलाने को चली आई है
मेरी महबूब, ये हंगामा-ए-तजदीदे-वफ़ा[9]
मेरी अफ़सुर्दा[10] जवानी के लिए रास नहीं

→

Apne sine se lagaye huye umeed ki lash
Muddaton zist ko nashad kiya hai maine
Tune to ek hi sadame se kiya tha do-chaar
Dil ko har tarah se barbaad kiya hai maine
Jab bhi rahon mein nazar aaye hariri-malboos
Sard aahon mein tujhe yaad kiya hai maine
Aur ab jabki meri rooh ke pahnai mein
Ek sunsaan-si maghmoom ghata chhai hai
Tu damkate huye aariz ki shuaayen lekar
Gulshuda shmyen jalane ko chali aai hai
Meri mahboob, ye hangama-e-tajdide-wafa
Meri afsurda jawani ke liye raas nahin

---

1. जीवन को 2. खिन्न, 3. रेशमी लिबास 4. आत्मा की विस्तीर्णता में 5. दुखी 6. कपोलों का 7. रश्मियां 8. बुझी हुई 9. प्रेम के नवीकरण का हंगामा 10. उदास, बुझी हुई

Defeat

Holding my dead hopes close to my chest
For long have I lived a life of misery
You gave me just a shock and left distraught
I have in every manner ruined my heart
And yet when I see somebody clad in silks
I sigh and remember you a lot
And now when sadness has completely enveloped
The vast expanse of my desolate heart
You, with the light of your glowing cheeks
Have come to relight a blown-out candle
This fanfare of renewed love, my dear
Suits not my ruined youth at all

→

मैंने जो फूल चुने थे तेरे क़दमों के लिए
उनका धुंधला-सा तसव्वुर [1] भी मेरे पास नहीं
एक यख़बस्ता [2] उदासी है दिलों-जां पे मुहीत [3]
अब मेरी रूह में बाक़ी है न उम्मीद न जोश
रह गया दब के गिरांबार सलासिल के [4] तले
मेरी दरमांदा [5] जवानी के उमंगों का ख़रोश [6]
रेगज़ारों में [7] बगूलों के सिवा कुछ भी नहीं
साया-ए-अब्रे-गुरेज़ां से [8] मुझे क्या लेना
बुझ चुके हैं मिरे सीने में मोहब्बत के कंवल
अब तिरे हुस्ने-पशेमां से [9] मुझे क्या लेना
तेरे आरिज़ पे ये ढलके हुए सीमी [10] आंसू
मेरी अफ़सुर्दगी-ए-ग़म का [11] मुदाबा [12] तो नहीं
तेरी महजूब निगाहों का [13] पयामे-तजदीद [14]
इकतलाफ़ी [15] ही सही मेरी तमन्ना तो नहीं

Maine jo phool chune the tere kadamon ke liye
Unka dhundhla-sa tasavvur bhi mere paas nahin
Ek yakhbasta udaasi hai dilon-jaan pe muheet
Ab meri rooh mein baki hai na umeed na josh
Rah gaya dab ke giranbar salaasil ke tale
Meri darmanda jawani ke umangon ka kharosh
Regzaron mein bagulon ke siwa kuchh bhi nahi
Saya-e-abre-gurezan se mujhe kya lena
Bujh chuke hain mire sine mein mohbbat ke kanwal
Ab tire husne-pasheman se mujhe kya lena
Tere aariz pe ye dhalke huye simi aansu
Meri afsurdgi-e-gham ka mudaba to nahin
Teri mahzoob nigahon ka payaame-tajdeed
Ik talafi hi sahi meri tamanna to nahin

---

1. कल्पना 2. बर्फ़ की तरह जमी हुई 3. छाई हुई 4. बोझिल ज़ंजीरों के 5. विवश 6. जोश 7. मरुस्थलों में 8. भागते हुए बादल की छाया से 9. लज्जित सौन्दर्य से 10. रजत 11. ग़म की उदासी का 12. इलाज 13. लज्जित नज़रों का 14. नवीकरण-संदेश 15. क्षतिपूर्ति

And I cannot even faintly recall
The flowers which I had picked up to spread under your feet
And now a benumbing sadness has covered my heart
I have neither hope, nor any spirit left
All my enthusiasm and hopes of youth
Lie buried under a heavy weight of chains in which I am caught
Now in these deserts there is nothing but whirlwinds
The shade of cool clouds is not meant for me
The blossoms of love in my heart are a withered lot
And your repentant beauty now suits me not
Now your cheeks and silken tresses
Cannot lift my sad, sad heart
And this renewed invitation from your repentant eyes
May be some compensation but forms not my desire's part

शहकार[1]

मुसव्विर[2]! मैं तिरा शहकार वापस करने आया हूं

अब इन रंगीन रुख़सारों में[3] थोड़ी ज़र्दियां भर दे
हिजाब-आलद[4] नज़रों में ज़रा बेबाकियां भर दे

लबों की[5] भीगी-भीगी सलवटों को मुज़्महिल[6] कर दे
नुमायां रंगे-पेशानी पे[7] अक्से-सोज़े-दिल[8] कर दे

तबस्सुम-आफ़री[9] चेहरे में कुछ संजीदापन भर दे
जवां सीने की मख़रूती[10] उठानें सरनिगूं[11] कर दे

घने बालों को कम कर दे मगर रुख़शिंदगी[12] दे दे
नज़र से तम्कनत[13] लेकर मज़ाके-आजिज़ी[14] दे दे

मगर हां बेंच के बदले इसे सोफ़े पे बिठला दे
यहां मेरी बजाय इक चमकती कार दिखला दे

Musvvir! main tira shahkar vapas karne aaya hon

Ab in rangeen rukhsaron mein thodi zardiyan bhar de
Hijab-aalad nazaron mein zara bebakiyan bhar de

Labon ki bhigi-bhigi salvaton ko muzmhil kar de
Numayan range-peshani pe akse-soze-dil kar de

Tabssum-aafari chehre mein kud sanjidapan bhar de
Jawan sine ki makhrooti uthane sarnigu kar de

Ghane balon ko kam kar de magar rukhshindgi de de
Nazar se tamknat lekar mazake-aajizi de de

Magar han bainch ke badale ise sofe pe bithla de
Yahan meri bajay ek chamkati car dikhla de

---

1. महान कलाकृति 2. चित्रकार 3. कपोलों में 4. लज्जाशील 5. होंठों की 6. व्याकुल 7. माथे के रंग पर 8. हृदय की जलन का प्रतिबिम्ब 9. मुस्कराते 10. गोल तथा नुकीली 11. झुकी हुई 12. चमक 13. अभिमान 14. विनयशीलता

Masterpiece

Painter, I have come to return your masterpiece
Put some paleness in these rosy cheeks
Instead of being shy make these eyes looking straight
Make the juicy lips dry and withered
And on the forehead
Instead of visible glow, paint sadness of the heart

Lend some seriousness to the face glowing with a
ravishing smile
Make the swelling breasts sinking low
And let the thick hair be thin and silver grey
Take away the shine in the eyes and put humility there
But instead of this bench, let her a sofa grace
And show a shining car standing here instead of me

कभी-कभी

कभी-कभी मेरे दिल में ख़याल आता है!

कि ज़िंदगी तेरी ज़ुल्फ़ों की नर्म छाओं में
गुज़रने पाती तो शादाब हो भी सकती थी
ये तीरगी[1] जो मेरी ज़ीस्त का मुक़द्दर[2] है
तेरी नज़र की शुआओ में[3] खो भी सकती थी

अजब न था कि मैं बेगाना-ए-अलम[4] रहकर
तिरे जमाल की[5] रानाइयों में[6] खो रहता
तिरा गुदाज़[7] बदन, तेरी नीम-बाज़[8] आंखें
इन्हीं हसीन फ़सानों में महव[9] हो रहता

→

Kabhi-kabhi mere dil mein khyaal aata hai!

Ki zindgi teri zulfon ki narm chhaon mein
Guzarne pati to shadab ho bhi sakti thi
Ye tirgi jo meri zist ka mukaddar hai
Teri nazar ki shuaao mein kho bhi sakti thi

Ajab na tha ki main begana-e-alam rahkar
Tire jamaal ki ranaiyon mein kho rahta
Tira gudaz badan, teri neem-baz aankhe
Inhi hasin fasanon mein mahv ho rahta

---

1. अंधेरा 2. जीवन का भाग्य 3. रश्मियों में 4. दुःखों में अपरिचित 5. सौन्दर्य की 6. लावण्यताओं में 7. मृदुल, कोमल 8. अधखुली 9. निमग्न

Sometime

Sometime, I tend to think
That my life, if it had passed under the cool shade of your tresses
Could very well have succeeded
And the gloom which has now become my fate
Could by the rays shooting from your eyes have been illuminated

It is quite possible that unmindful of the world around
I could have lost myself in the realms of your beauty
And could have remained immersed
In the lore of your half-shut eyes and soft filled-up body

→

पुकारतीं मुझे जब तल्ख़ियां ज़माने की
मेरे लबों से[1] हलावत[2] के घूंट पी लेता
हयात[3] चीख़ती-फिरती बरहना-सर[4] और मैं
घनेरी ज़ुल्फ़ों के साए में छुप के जी लेता

मगर ये हो न सका और अब ये आलम[5] है
कि तू नहीं, तेरा ग़म, तेरी जुस्तजू भी नहीं
गुज़र रही है कुछ इस तरह ज़िंदगी जैसे
इसे किसी के सहारे की आरज़ू भी नहीं

ज़माने भर के दुखों को लगा चुका हूं गले
गुज़र रहा हूं कुछ अनजानी गुज़रगाहों से
मुहीब[6] साए मेरी सम्त बढ़ते आते हैं
हयातों-मौत[7] के पुर-हौल ख़ारज़ारों से[8]

→

Pukartin mujhe jab talkhiyan zamane ki
Mere labon se halaawat ke ghunt pi leta
Hayaat chikhati-phirti barhana-sar aur mein
Ghaneri zulfon ke saye mein chhup ke ji leta

Magar ye ho na saka aur ab ye aalam hai
Ki tu nahin, tera gham, teri justju bhi nahin
Guzar rahi hai kuchh is tarah zindgi jaise
Ise kisi ke sahare ki aarzoo bhi nahin

Zamane bhar ke dukhon ko laga chuka hun gale
Guzar raha hun kuchh anjani guzargahon se
Muhib saye meri samt badte aate hain
Hayaton-maut ke pur-haul khajzaron se

---

1. होंठों से 2. माधुर्य, रस 3. जीवन 4. नंगे सिर 5. स्थिति 6. भयानक 7. जीवन तथा मृत्यु 8. भयावह कंटीले जंगलों से

It is possible that when the bitter realities were beckoning me
And life was howling around with its head bare
I could have lived oblivious of it all
Under the thick dark shades of your hair

But that was not to be, and now
Neither are you with me, nor your grief nor do I seek for you
And my life is passing in such a way
That now without anybody I can live

Sorrows of the whole world I have embraced
And am passing through unfamiliar ways
Horrifying shadows are moving towards me
From the dreadful forest from where death-in-life on me preys

→

न कोई जादह[1] न मंज़िल न रौशनी का सुराग़
भटक रही है ख़लाओं में[2] ज़िंदगी मेरी
इन्हीं खलाओं में रह जाऊंगा कभी खोकर
मैं जानता हूं मेरी हम-नफ़स[3] मगर यूंही

कभी-कभी मेरे दिल में ख़याल आता है!

Na koi jadah na manzil na roshani ka suraag
Bhatak rahi hai khalayon mein zindgi meri
Inhin khalayon mein rah jaoonga kabhi khokar
Main janta hun meri hum-nafas magar yunhi

Kabhi-kabhi mere dil mein khyal aata hai!

---

1. मार्ग 2. शून्यों में 3. सहचर

Neither a road opens for me, nor is there a destination, nor light
My life is passing through empty spaces
And in these spaces one day I will sink
I know it well but still
Sometime I tend to think

चकले

ये कूचे ये नीलामघर दिलकशी के
ये लुटते हुए कारवां ज़िंदगी के
कहां हैं? कहां हैं मुहाफ़िज़ खुदी[1] के
सना-ख़्वाने-तक़्दीसे-मशरिक़[2] कहां हैं?

ये पुरपेच गलियां, ये बेख़्वाब[3] बाज़ार
ये गुमनाम राही, ये सिक्कों की झनकार
ये इस्मत[4] के सौदे, ये सौदों पे तकरार
सना-ख़्वाने-तक़्दीसे-मशरिक़ कहां हैं?

तअफ़्फुन[5] से पुर नीम-रोशन[6] ये गलियां
ये मसली हुई अधखिली ज़र्द कलियां
ये बिकती हुई खोखली रंगरलियां
सना-ख़्वाने-तक़्दीसे-मशरिक़ कहां हैं?

→

Ye kuche ye nilamghar dilkashi ke
Ye lutte huye karwan zindgi ke
Kahan hain? kahan hain muhafiz khudi ke
Sana-khwane-takdise-mashrik kahan hain?

Ye purpech galiyan, ye bekhwab bazar
Ye gumnaam rahi, ye sikkon ki jhankar
Ye ismat ke saude, ye saudon pe takrar
Sana-khwane-takdise-mashrik kahan hain?

Taaffun se pur neem-roshan ye galiyan
Ye masali hui adhkhili zard kaliyan
Ye bikti hui khokhali rangraliyan
Sana-khwane-takdise-mashrik kahan hain?

---

1. अहं के रक्षक 2. पूर्व की पवित्रता के गुण गाने वाले 3. निद्रा-रहित 4. सतीत्व 5. दुर्गन्ध 6. मद्धम प्रकाश वाली

Brothel houses

These lanes, these auction houses selling entertainment
These caravans of life being openly looted
Where are the custodians of nation's honour
Where are those who pride themselves on the
superiority of the eastern culture!

These zigzag lanes, these ever awake busy bazaars
These unknown customers, these sounds of coins
ringing
This haggling here, these bargains of honour
Where are those who pride themselves on eastern
culture?

These hapless streets that have not slept for ages
These semi-blossomed buds crushed and pale
These romances hollow on sale for ever
Where are those who pride themselves on eastern
culture?

→

वो उजले दरीचों में पायल की छन-छन
तनफ़्फ़ुस[1] की उलझन पे तबले की धन-धन
ये बेरूह कमरों में खांसी की ढन-ढन
सना-ख़्वाने-तक़्दीसे-मशरिक़ कहां हैं?

ये गूंजे हुए क़हक़हे रास्तों पर
ये चारों तरफ़ भीड़-सी खिड़कियों पर
ये आवाज़ें खिंचते हुए आंचलों पर
सना-ख़्वाने-तक़्दीसे-मशरिक़ कहां हैं?

ये फूलों के गजरे, ये पीकों के छींटे
ये बेबाक नज़रें, ये गुस्ताख़ फ़िक़रे
ये ढलके बदन और ये मदक़ूक़[2] चेहरे
सना-ख़्वाने-तक़्दीसे-मशरिक़ कहां हैं?

→

Wo ujale darichon mein payal ki chhan-chhan
Taaffus ki uljhan pe table ki dhan-dhan
Ye berooh kamaron mein khansi ki dan-dan
Sana-khwane-takdise-mashrik kahan hain?

Ye goonje huye kahkahe raston par
Ye charon taraf bheed-si khidkiyon par
Ye aawazen khinchte huye aanchalon par
Sana-khwane-takdise-mashrik kahan hain?

Ye phoolon ke gajare, ye pikon ke chhinte
Ye bebaak nazarein, ye gustakh fikare
Ye dalke badan aur ye madkook chehre
Sana-khwane-takdise-mashrik kahan hain?

---

1. श्वास 2. क्षयग्रस्त

The sound of anklets ringing through the well-lit windows
The tabla playing alongside the breaking breath
These bouts of cough, these lifeless rooms here
Where are those who pride themselves on eastern culture?

This laughter on the pathways noisy
These crowds gathered around the windows everywhere
These maidens being pulled at amid obscene calls clear
Where are those who pride themselves on eastern culture!

These flower bands, these stains of spit from paan-chewing
These shameless eyes, these utterances annoying
These bodies crumbling, these sickly faces
Where are those who pride themselves on eastern culture?

→

ये भूखी निगाहें हसीनों की जानिब
ये बढ़ते हुए हाथ सीनों की जानिब
लपकते हुए पांव ज़ीनों की जानिब
सना-ख़्वाने-तक़्दीसे-मशरिक़ कहां हैं?

यहां पीर[1] भी आ चुके हैं जवां भी
तनूमंद[2] बेटे भी अब्बा मियां भी
ये बीबी भी है और बहन भी है मां भी
सना-ख़्वाने-तक़्दीसे-मशरिक़ कहां हैं?

Ye bhookhi nigahein haseenon ki janib
Ye badte huye hath seenon ki janib
Lapkate huye paon zeenon ki janib
Sana-khwane-takdise-mashrik kahan hain?

Yahan peer bhi aa chuke hain jawan bhi
Tanumand bete bhi abba miyan bhi
Ye bibi bhi hai aur bahan bhi hai maan bhi
Sana-khwane-takdise-mashrik kahan hain?

---

1. बूढ़े 2. हृष्ट-पुष्ट

These hungry eyes devouring pretty faces
These hands advancing towards the breasts
These feet hastening towards the stairs
Where are those who pride themselves on eastern culture?

These bazaars visited both by young and old alike
The strapping sons, the fathers revered
These women are mothers, wives as well as sisters
Where are those who pride themselves on the superiority of the eastern culture?

मुझे सोचने दे!

मेरी नाकाम मोहब्बत की कहानी मत छेड़
अपनी मासूम उमंगों का फ़साना न सुना
ज़िंदगी तल्ख़ सही, ज़हर[1] सही, ग़म ही सही
दर्दो-आज़ार[2] सही, जब्र सही, ग़म ही सही
लेकिन इस दर्दो-ग़मो-जब्र[3] की वुसअत[4] को तो देख
ज़ुल्म की छांओं में दम तोड़ती ख़लक़त को तो देख
अपनी मायूस उमंगों का फ़साना न सुना
मेरी नाकाम मोहब्बत की कहानी मत छेड़

जल्सागाहों में ये दहशत-ज़दा[5] सहमे अंबोह[6]
रहगुज़ारों पे फलाकत-ज़दा[7] लोगों के गिरोह
भूख और प्यास से पज़मुर्दा[8] सियहफ़ाम[9] ज़मीं

→

Meri nakaam mohabbat ki kahani mat chhed
Apni masoom umangon ka fasana na suna
Zindgi talkh sahi, zahar sahi, gham hi sahi
Dardo-aazar sahi, jabra sahi, gham hi sahi
Lekin is dardo-ghamo-jabra ki vusat ko to dekh
Zulm ki chhaon mein dam todti khalkat ko to dekh
Apni mayoos umangon ka fasana na suna
Meri nakaam mohabbat ki kahani mat chhed

Jalsagahon mein ye dahshat-zada sahme amboh
Rahguzaron pe falaakat-zada logon ke giroh
Bhookh aur pyaas se pazmurda siyahfam zameen

---

1. विष 2. पीड़ा तथा रोग 3. दर्द, ग़म, अत्याचार 4. फैलाव 5. आतंकित 6. जन-समूह 7. निर्धनता के मारे हुए 8. म्लान 9. काली

Let me think

Do not tell me tale of my failed love
Let me not hear the litany of your defeated desires
Life may be bitter, it may poison itself
It may be full of pain, cruelty and suffering though
You must see the vastness of this cruelty and suffering
See the multitudes dying under tyranny
Let me not hear the litany of your defeated desires
Do not tell me the tale of my failed love

These terrorised crowds in the public meetings
These crumbling millions everywhere
Hunger and thirst have made the earth lifeless and
bleak

→

तीरहो-तार मकां[1] मुफ़्लिसो-बीमार मकीं[2]
नौ-ए-इन्सां में[3] ये सरमाया-ओ-मेहनत[4] का तज़ाद[5]
अम्नो-तहज़ीब के परचम तले क़ौमों का फ़साद
हर तरफ़ आतिशो-आहन का[6] ये सैलाबे-अज़ीम[7]
नित नये तर्ज़ पे होती हुई दुनिया तक़सीम

लहलहाते हुए खेतों पे जवानी का समां
और दहक़ान[8] के छप्पर में न बत्ती न धुआं
ये फ़लक-बोस[9] मिलें, दिलकशो-सीमी[10] बाज़ार
ये ग़लाज़त[11] पे झपटते हुए भूके नादार
दूर साहिल पे वो शफ़्फ़ाफ़[12] मकानों की क़तार
सरसराते हुए पर्दों में सिमटते गुलज़ार[13]

→

Teerho-taar makaa mufliso-bimaar makeen
Nau-e-insaan mein ye sarmaya-o-mehnat ka tazaad
Amno-tagzeeb ke parcham tale kaumon ka fasaad
Har tarah aatisho-aahan ka ye sailabe-azeem
Nit naye tarz pe hoti hui duniya takseem

Lahlahate huye kheton pe jawani ka samaan
Aur dahkaan ke chhappar mein batti na dhuaan
Ye falak-bos milen, dilkasho-simi bazar
Pe galaazat pe jhapte huye bhooke nadar
Door sahil pe vo shaffak makanon ke kataar
Sarsarate huye pardon mein simatte gulzaar

---

1. तंग तथा अंधेरे मकान, 2. वासी, 3. मनुष्य, 4. पूंजी तथा श्रम, 5. संघर्ष, टकराव, 6. आग और लोहे का, 7. महान बाढ़ 8. किसान 9. गगनचुम्बी 10. सुन्दर और रजत 11. गन्दगी 12. उज्ज्वल 13. पुष्प-वाटिकाएं

See the dark, dingy houses and their impoverished sickly residents
See the clash of labour and capital in the world
The conflict among nations under the banners of peace and civilised conduct
The flood of fire and steel everywhere
And the division of the world in novel way everyday

See the glorious green fields at their prime
And in the farmer's hut neither light nor smoke
See these skyscrapers, these lovely decorated bazaars
This dirt, these poor people pouncing on anything
And a row of glittering houses on the sea shore at some distance
The flower pots get covered by the wind swept curtains

→

दरो-दीवार पे अनवार का[1] सैलाबे-रवां[2]
जैसे इक शायरे-मदहोश[3] के ख़्वाबों का जहां
ये सब क्यों है? ये क्या है? मुझे कुछ सोचने दे
कौन इन्सां .ख़ुदा है, मुझे कुछ सोचने दे
अपनी मायूस उमंगों का फ़साना न सुना
मेरी नाकाम मोहब्बत की कहानी मत छेड़

Daro-diwar pe anwar ka sailabe-rawan
Jaise ek shaayare-madhosh ke khwabon ka jahan
Ye sab kyon hai? ye kya hai? mujhe kuchh sochane de
Kaun insaan khuda hai, mujhe kuchh sochane de
Apni mayoos umangon ka fasana na suna
Meri nakaam mohabbat ki kahani mat chhed

---

1. प्रकाश का 2. बहती बाढ़ 3. मदहोश शायर

And the walls and ceilings in flood light bathed
Like the dream world of an intoxicated poet
What is all this? why is it all there? let me think
Who is our God here let me think
Let me not hear the litany of your defeated desires
Do not tell me the tale of my failed love

तेरी आवाज़

रात सुनसान थी, बोझिल थी फ़ज़ा की सांसें
रूह पे छाए थे बेनाम ग़मों के साए
दिल को ये ज़िद थी कि तू आए तसल्ली देने
मेरी कोशिश थी कि कमबख़्त को नींद आ जाए

देर तक आंखों में चुभती रही तारों की चमक
देर तक ज़ेहन सुलगता रहा तन्हाई में
अपने ठुकराए हुए दोस्त की पुरसिश[1] के लिए
तू न आई मगर इस रात की पहनाई[2] में

यूं अचानक तेरी आवाज़ कहीं से आई
जैसे परबत का जिगर चीर के झरना फूटे
या ज़मीनों की मोहब्बत में तड़प कर नागाह
आसमानों से कोई शोख़ सितारा टूटे

→

Raat sunsaan thi, bojhil thi faza ki sansen
Rooh pe chhaye the benaam ghamon ke saye
Dil ko ye zid thi ki tu aaye tasalli dene
Meri koshish thi ki kambakht ko neend aa jaye

Der tak aankhon mein chubhti rahi taron ki chamak
Der tak zehan sulgata raha tanhai mein
Apne thukraye huye dost ki pursish ke liye
Tu na aai magar is raat ki pahnaai mein

Yun achanak teri aawaz kahin se aai
Jaise parbat ka jigar cheer ke jharna phoote
Ya zameeno ki mohabbat mein tadap kar nagah
aasmanon se koi shokh sitara toote

---

1. हाल-चाल पूछना 2. विशालता

Your voice

The night was desolate and the atmosphere heavy
Nameless sorrows oppressed my heart
Which yearned for you to come and comfort it
While my effort was to put the silly thing to sleep

For long did the moonlight hurt the eyes
For long the mind burned in loneliness
But on that endless lonely night
You came not to console your friend

Then suddenly like a spring gushing out of a rock
Or like a star mad with love for the earth
Falling from the sky
I heard your voice coming from somewhere

→

शहद-सा घुल गया तल्ख़ाबा-ए-तन्हाई में[1]
रंग-सा फैल गया दिल के सियाह-ख़ाने में
देर तक यूं तेरी मस्ताना सदायें गूंजीं
जिस तरह फूल चटकने लगें वीराने में

तू बहुत दूर किसी अंजुमने-नाज़ में थी
फिर भी महसूस किया मैंने कि तू आई है
और नग़्मों में छुपाकर मेरे खोए हुए ख़्वाब
मेरी रूठी हुई नींदों को मना लाई है

रात की सतह पे उभरे तेरे चेहरे के नुक़ूश[2]
वही चुपचाप-सी आंखें वही सादा-सी नज़र
वही ढलका हुआ आंचल, वही रफ़्तार का ख़म[3]
वही रह-रह के लचकता हुआ नाज़ुक पैकर[4]

→

Shahd-sa ghul gaya talkhaba-e-tanhai mein
Rang-sa phail gaya dil ke siyah-khane mein
Der tak yun teri mastana sadayein goonjin
Jis tarah phool chatkane lagein virane mein

Tu bahut door kisi anjumane-naaz mein thi
Phir bhi mahsoos kiya maine ki tu aai hai
Aur nagmon mein chhupakar mere khoye huye khwab
Meri roothi hui neendon ko mana laai hai

Raat ki satah pe ubhare tere chehre ki nukoosh
Wahi chupchaap-si aankhe wahi sada-si nazar
Wahi dalka hua aanchal, wahi raftaar ka kham
Wahi rah-rah ke lachakta hua nazuk paikar

---

1. एकान्त के कड़वेपन में 2. नैन-नक़्श 3. चाल की लचक 4. बदन

The bitter unbearable loneliness become sweet
The gloom in the heart suddenly got illuminated
And like the buds opening up in a desert land
Your intoxicating voice kept ringing in my ears

It felt that from a far-off fairy land you came
And concealing my lost sleep in your songs
Brought it into my eyes

The same simple silent eyes
The same headcover hanging, the same winsome gait
The same delicate physical frame
Floating before my eyes that night came

→

तू मेरे पास न थी फिर भी सहर[1] होने तक
तेरी हर सांस मेरे जिस्म को छूकर गुज़री
क़तरा-क़तरा तेरे दीदार[2] की शबनम टपकी
लम्हा-लम्हा तेरी ख़ुशबू से मुअत्तर[3] गुज़रा

अब यही है तुझे मंज़ूर तो ऐ जाने-बहार[4]
मैं तेरी राह न देखूंगा सियाह रातों में
ढूंढ लेंगी मेरी तरसी हुई नज़रें तुझको
नग़्मा-ओ-शे'र की उमड़ी हुई बरसातों में

अब तेरा प्यार सताएगा तो मेरी हस्ती
तेरी मस्ती भरी आवाज़ में ढल जाएगी
और ये रूह जो तेरे लिए बेचैन-सी है
गीत बनकर तेरे होंटों प मचल जाएगी

→

Tu mere paas na thi phir bhi sahar hone tak
Teri har saans mere jism ko chhukar guzaraa
Katra-katra tere deedar ki shabnam tapki
Lamha-lamha teri kḥushboo se muattar guzaraa

Ab yahi hai tujhe manzoor to ye jaane-bahaar
Main teri raah na dekhunga siyah raaton mein
Doond lengi meri tarsi hui nazarein tujhko
Nagma-o-sher ki umadi hui barsaaton mein

Ab tera pyaar satayega to meri hasti
Teri masti bhari aawaz mein dhal jayegi
Aur ye rooh jo tere liye bechain-si hai
Geet bankar tere honto pe machal jayegi

---

1. सुबह 2. दर्शन 3. सुगन्धित 4. बहारों की जान (प्रिया)

You were not by my side though, still till the dawn
Your breath kissed my body as it passed
With every moment fragrant with your presence
I saw your every bit last night

If this is what you want, let it be, my dear
I will not look forward to meeting you in the thick dark nights
But remember, your longing eye will look for me everywhere
And you will miss pleasures of my song and poetry

Now on, whenever I am troubled by your spell-binding love
My life will replicate your voice
And my soul which is ever yearning for you
Will become a song on your lips

→

तेरे नग़्मात, तेरे हुस्न की ठंडक लेकर
मेरे तपते हुए माहौल में आ जाएंगे
चन्द घड़ियों के लिए हो कि हमेशा के लिए
मेरी जागी हुई रातों को सुला जाएंगे

Tere nagmaat, tere husn ki thandak lekar
Mere tapte huye mahaul mein aa jayenge
Chand ghadiyon ke liye ho ki hamesha ke liye
Meri jaagi hui ratoon ko sula jayenge

The coolth of your beauty and song
Will cool my scalding environments too
And those few moments will become for me eternal
And make the rest of my nights supremely peaceful

मता-ए-ग़ैर[1]

मेरे ख़्वाबों के झरोखों को सजानेवाली
तेरे ख़्वाबों में कहीं मेरा गुज़र है कि नहीं
पूछकर अपनी निगाहों से बता दे मुझको
मेरी रातों के मुक़द्दर[2] में सहर[3] है कि नहीं

चार दिन की ये रफ़ाक़त[4] जो रफ़ाक़त भी नहीं
उम्र भर के लिए आज़ार[5] हुई जाती है
ज़िंदगी यूं तो हमेशा से परेशान-सी थी
अब तो हर सांस गिरां-बार[6] हुई जाती है

मेरी उजड़ी हुई नींदों के शबिस्तानों में[7]
तू किसी ख़्वाब के पैकर[8] की तरह आई है
कभी अपनी-सी, कभी ग़ैर नज़र आती है
कभी इख़्लास[9] की मूरत, कभी हरजाई है

→

Mere khwaboon ke jharokhon ko sajanewali
Tere khwaboon mein kahin mera guzar hai ki nahin
Poochhkar apni nigahon se bata de mujhko
Meri raaton ke mukaddar mein sahar hai ki nahin

Chaar din ki ye rafaakat jo rafaakat bhi nahin
Umr bhar ke liye aazar hui jati hai
Zindgi yun to hamesha se pareshan-si thi
Ab to har saans giran-baar hui jati hai

Meri ujari hui neendon ke shabistanon mein
Tu kisi khwab ke paikar ki tarah aai hai
Kabhi apni-si, kabhi gair nazar aati hai
Kabhi ikhlaas ki murat, kabhi harjaai hai

---

1. ग़ैर की सम्पत्ति 2. भाग्य 3. प्रभात 4. साथ 5. रोग 6. असह्य, बोझिल 7. शयनागारों में 8. शरीर, 9. निःस्वार्थता

Somebody else's wealth

You, who have lit up my dreams
Do I ever pass your dreams too
Ask your eyes and let me know
Will my nights ever see the dawn or not

This companionship which is hardly a companionship
Is now becoming a life-long agony
Life has always been a sorry affair
But now every breath is becoming an unbearable burden

In my sleepless barren nights
You have sometime come as a dream embodied
Sometime as my own sometime like a stranger
You have looked sometime unfaithful, sometime a picture of sacrifice

→

प्यार पर बस तो नहीं है मिरा, लेकिन फिर भी
तू बता दे कि तुझे प्यार करूं या न करूं
तूने ख़ुद अपने तबस्सुम से[1] जगाया है जिन्हें
उन तमन्नाओं का इज़्हार[2] करूं या न करूं

तू किसी और के दामन की कली है, लेकिन
मेरी रातें तेरी ख़ुशबू से बसी रहती हैं
तू कहीं भी हो तेरे फूल-से आरिज़ की[3] क़सम
तेरी पलकें मेरी आंखों पे झुकी रहती हैं

तेरे हाथों की हरारत[4], तेरे सांसों की महक
तैरती रहती है एहसास की[5] पहनाई में[6]
ढूंढती रहती हैं तख़ईल की[7] बांहें तुझको
सर्द रातों की सुलगती हुई तन्हाई में

→

Pyaar par bas to nahi hai mira, lekin phir bhi
Tu bata de ki tujhe pyaar karoon ya na karoon
Tune khud apne tabssum se jagaya hai jinhe
Un tamannaon ka izhaar karoon ya na karoon

Tu kisi aur ke daman ki kali hai, lekin
Meri raatein teri khushboo se basi rahti hain
Tu kahin bhi ho tere phool-se aariz ki kasam
Teri palakein meri aankon pe jhuki rahati hain

Tere hathon ki haraarat, tere saanson ki mahak
Tairti rahati hai ahsaas ki pahnaai mein
Doondti rahati hain takhail ki banhein tujhko
Sard raaton ki sulgati hui tanhai mein

---

1. मुस्कुराहट से 2. प्रकटन 3. गालों की 4. गर्मी 5. अनुभूति की 6. विस्तीर्णता में
7. कल्पना की

I have no control over my love, but still
Tell me whether I should love you or not
And express a longing in my heart
Which you kindled with your smile

You are a bud, meant to deck somebody else's apparel
But your fragrance fills my nights
Wherever you may be, I swear by your flower-like cheeks
Your eyes are always bent on my eyes

The warmth of your hands, the fragrance of your breath
Is ever permeating the very depth of my feelings
In the scalding solitariness of cold nights
My imagination is ever yearning to take you in its arms

→

तेरा अल्ताफ़ो-करम[1] एक हक़ीक़त[2] है, मगर
ये हक़ीक़त भी हक़ीक़त में फ़साना[3] ही न हो
तेरी मानूस निगाहों का[4] ये मोहतात पयाम
दिल के ख़ूं करने का एक और बहाना ही न हो

कौन जाने मिरे इम्रोज़ का[5] फ़र्दा[6] क्या है
क़ुर्बतें[7] बढ़ के पशेमान[8] भी हो जाती हैं
दिल के दामन से लिपटते हुई रंगीं नजरें
देखते-देखते अनजान भी हो जाती हैं

मेरी दरमांदा[9] जवानी की तमन्नाओं के
मुज़्महिल[10] ख़्वाब की ता'बीर[11] बता दे मुझको
तेरे दामन में गुलिस्तां भी हैं, वीराने भी
मेरा हासिल[12] मेरी तक़्दीर बता दे मुझको

Tera altafo-karam ek hakikat hai, magar
Ye hakikat bhi hakikat mein fasana hi na ho
Teri maanus nigahon ka ye mohtaat payaam
Dil ke khoon karane ka ek aur bahana hi na ho

Kaun jane mire imroz ka farda kya hai
Kurbate badke pashemaan bhi ho jati hain
Dil ke daman se liptte huye rangin nazarein
Dekhte-dekhte anjaan bhi ho jati hain

Meri darmanda jawani ki tamannaon ke
Muzmhil khwab ki taabir bataa de mujhko
Tere daman mein gulistan bhi hain, virane bhi
Mera hasil meri takdeer bataa de mujhko

---

1. कृपा, अनुकम्पा 2. वास्तविकता 3. कहानी 4. इष्ट नज़रों का 5. आज का 6. कल 7. सामीप्य, प्रेम 8. लज्जित 9. विवश 10. आकुल 11. स्वप्न फल 12. प्राप्ति

Your kindness to me is a reality, of course
But I fear lest this reality turn into fiction
And the lovely message from your lovely eyes
Should become a messenger of my death

Who knows my today will see its tomorrow or not
You who are so close to me can from me withdraw too
And the eyes enveloping my heart now
Can in no time into strangers turn

Do let me know what is in store
For the dreams of my restless youth
You who can for me a garden or wilderness create
Please tell me what shall I get, what will be my fate

एक मंज़र

उफ़ुक़ के[1] दरीचे से किरणों ने झांका
फ़ज़ा[2] तन गई रास्ते मुस्कराए
सिमटने लगी नर्म कुहरे की चादर
जवां शाख़सारों ने[3] घूंघट उठाए
परिन्दों की आवाज़ से खेत चौंके
पुर-असरार[4] लय में रहट गुनगुनाए
हसीं शबनम-आलूद[5] पगडण्डियों से
लिपटने लगे सब्ज़ पेड़ों के साए

वो दूर एक टीले पे आंचल-सा झलका
तसव्वुर में[6] लाखों दिये झिलमिलाए

Ufuk ke dariche se kiranon ne jhanka
Faza tan gai raste muskaraye
Simtane lagi narm kuhare ki chaadar
Jawan shakhsaron ne ghunghat Uthaye
Parindon ki aawaz se khet chaunke
Pur-asraar lay mein rahat gungunaye
Hasin shabnam-aalud pagdandiyon se
Liptne lage sabz pedon ke saye

Wo door ek teele pe aanchal-sa jhalaka
Tasvvur mein lakhon diye jhilmilaye

---

1. क्षितिज के 2. वातावरण 3. जवान वृक्ष-पुंजों ने 4. रहस्यपूर्ण 5. ओस-भरी 6. कल्पना में

A scene

The rays of the sun peeped through the horizon's window
The atmosphere came alive and the pathway smiled
The fog started gradually receding
And the green groves their veils lifted
The noise of the birds woke up the fields
And the Persian wheel started humming an inviting tune
And the shadows of the trees started embracing the dew-covered by-ways
On a far-off hillock an 'aanchal' is sighted
And my fancy has a thousand candles lighted

ख़ाना-आबादी

(एक दोस्त की शादी पर)

तराने गूंज उठे हैं फ़ज़ा में शादियानों के
हवा है इत्र-आगी[1], ज़र्रा-ज़र्रा मुस्कराता है

मगर दूर एक अफ़सुर्दा[2] मकां में सर्द बिस्तर पर
कोई दिल है कि हर आहट पे यूं ही चौंक जाता है

मेरी आंखों में आंसू आ गए 'नादीदह आंखों' के[3]
मेरे दिल में कोई ग़मग़ीन नग़्मा सरसराता है

ये रस्मे-इन्क़िताए-अहदे-उल्फ़त[4], ये हयाते-नौ[5]
मोहब्बत रो रही है, और तमद्दुन[6] मुस्कराता है

ये शादी ख़ाना-आबादी हो, मेरे मोहतरिम[7] भाई
'मुबारक' कह नहीं सकता, मेरा दिल कांप जाता है

Tarane goonj uthe hain faza mein shaadiyanon ke
Hawa hai itra-aagi, zara-zara muskarata hai

Magar door ek afsurda makaan mein sard bistar par
Koi dil hai ki har aahat pe yun hi chaunk jata hai

Meri aankhon mein aansu aa gaye nadidah aankhon ke
Mere dil mein koi ghamgeen naghma sarsarata hai

Ye rasme-inkitaye-ahade-ulfat ye hayate-nau
Mohabbat ro rahi hai, aur tamddun muskarata hai

Ye shaadi khana-aabadi ho, mere mohtarimbhai
'Mubarak' kah nahin sakta, mera dil kaanp jata hai

---

1. सुगन्धित 2. उदास 3. अनदेखी आंखों के 4. प्रेम-काल की समाप्ति की रीति 5. नवजीवन 6. संस्कृति 7. आदरणीय

Setting up home
(On a friend's wedding)

Wedding songs are echoing in the air
And the atmosphere is filled with fragrant smiles

At some distance however, a sad heart in a sad house
Startles up at every sound

My eyes are brimming with tears of unseen eyes
And a melancholy song wells up from the heart

Love weeps and culture smiles
Over this quitting of old love for the new

This marriage will destroy a house, my brother dear
So I cannot congratulate, my heart sinks, I fear

फ़नकार[1]

मैंने जो गीत तेरे प्यार की ख़ातिर लिखे
आज उन गीतों को बाज़ार में ले आया हूं

आज दूकान पे नीलाम उठेगा उनका
तूने जिन गीतों पे रक्खी थी मोहब्बत की असास[2]
आज चांदी की तराज़ू में तुलेगी हर चीज़
मेरे अफ़कार[3], मेरी शायरी, मेरा एहसास

जो तेरी ज़ात से मनसूब[4] थे उन गीतों को
मुफ़्लिसी जिन्स[5] बनाने पे उतर आई है
भूख, तेरे रुख़े-रंगीं के[6] फ़सानों के इवज़
चन्द अशिया-ए-ज़रूरत की[7] तमन्नाई है

→

Meine jo geet tere pyaar ki khatir likhe
Aaj un geeton ko bazar mein le aaya hun

Aaj dukan pe nilaam uthega unka
Tune jin geeton pe rakhi thi mohabbat ki asaas
Aaj chandi ki tarazoo mein tulegi har cheez
Mere afkaar, meri shayari, mera ahsaas

Jo teri zaat se mansoob the un geeton ko
Muflisi jins banane pe utar aai hai
Bhookh, tere rukhe-rangin ke fasanon ke ivaz
Chand ashiya-e-zaroorat ki tamannai hai

---

1. कलाकार 2. नींव 3. रचनाएं 4. सम्बन्धित 5. खाद्य-पदार्थ 6. रंगीन चेहरे के 7. ज़रूरत की चीज़ों की

The artist

The songs of love that I wrote for you
Today I have brought them for sale in the market place

Today, I will put those songs on auction
Which are the foundation of your love for me
My feelings, my poetry, my creativity
Will all be weighed on the silver scale

My poverty compels me to turn into a commodity
The songs which I wrote for you specifically
I need the necessities of life which satisfy my hunger
More than the odes on your lovely face

→

देख इस अर्सागहे-मेहनतो-सर्माया[1] में
मेरे नग़्मे भी मेरे पास नहीं रह सकते
तेरे जलवे किसी ज़रदार[2] की मीरास सही
तेरे ख़ाके[3] भी मेरे पास नहीं रह सकते

आज उन गीतों को बाज़ार में ले आया हूं
मैंने जो गीत तेरे प्यार की ख़ातिर लिखे

Dekh is arsaagahe-mehnato-sarmaya mein
Mere nagme bhi mere paas nahin rah sakte
Tere jalwe kisi zardaar ki meeras sahi
Tere khake bhi mere paas nahin rah sakte

Aaj un geeton ko bazar mein le aaya hun
Maine jo geet tere pyaar ki khatir likhe

---

1. मेहनत और पूंजी के युद्ध-क्षेत्र में 2. पूंजीपति 3. रेखाचित्र

In this conflict between labour and capital
Even my songs I cannot for myself retain
Your beauty may be for somebody else earmarked
Even your sketches cannot with me remain

The songs of love that I wrote for you
Today I have brought them for sale to the market place

सोचता हूं

सोचता हूं कि मोहब्बत से किनारा कर लूं
दिल को बेगाना-ए-तरग़ीबो-तमन्ना[1] कर लूं

सोचता हूं कि मोहब्बत है जुनूने-रुसवा[2]
चंद बेकार-से बेहूदा ख़्यालों का हुजूम
एक आज़ाद को पाबन्द बनाने की हवस
एक बेगाने को अपनाने की सइए-मौहूम[3]

सोचता हूं कि मोहब्बत है सरूरो-मस्ती
इसकी तनवीर से[4] रौशन है फ़ज़ाए-हस्ती[5]

सोचता हूं कि मोहब्बत है बशर की फ़ितरत[6]
इसका मिट जाना, मिटा देना बहुत मुश्किल है

→

Sochata hun ki mohabbat se kinara kar loon
Dil ko begana-e-targeebo-tamanna kar loon

Sochata hoon ki mohabbat hai juncone-ruswa
Chand bekar-se behuda khyalon ka hujoom
Ek Aazad ko paband banane ki hawas
Ek begane ko apnane ki saiye-Mauhoom

Sochata hoon ki mohabbat hai sarooro-masti
Iski tanveer se roshan hai fazaye-hasti

Sochata hoon ki mohabbat hai bashar ki fitrat
Iska mit jana, mita dena bahut mushkil hai

---

1. अभिलाषा तथा प्रेरणा-रहित 2. बदनाम उन्माद 3. भ्रमात्मक प्रयत्न 4. प्रकाश से 5. जीवन का वातावरण 6. मानव का स्वभाव

I feel

Overcoming all inclination and desire for it
I sometime feel like turning my back on love

It sometime appears to me to be a useless
infatuation
A swarm of silly thoughts
An instrument of enslaving a free man
Or an illusory attempt at winning over a stranger

But then sometime I feel that love is a source of joy,
of ecstasy,
In the darkness of life, it is light;

Love is ingrained in human nature,
A candle you cannot easily blow out

→

सोचता हूं कि मोहब्बत से है ताबिंदा[1] हयात[2]
अब ये शम्अ बुझा देना बहुत मुश्किल है

सोचता हूं कि मोहब्बत पे कड़ी शर्तें हैं
इस तमद्दुन में[3] मसर्रत पे बड़ी शर्तें हैं

सोचता हूं कि मोहब्बत है इक अफ़सुर्दा[4]-सी लाश
चादरे-इज़्ज़तो-नामूस में[5] कफ़नाई हुई
दौरे-सर्माया[6] की रौंदी हुई रुसवा हस्ती
दरगहे-मज़हबो-इख़्लाक़ से[7] ठुकराई हुई

सोचता हूं कि बशर[8] और मोहब्बत का जुनूं
ऐसे बोसीदा तमद्दुन से है इक कारे-ज़बूं[9]

→

Sochata hoon ki mohabbat se hai tabinda hayaat
Ab ye shma bujha dena bahut mushkil hai.

Sochata hoon ki mohabbat pe kari shartein hain
Is tamddun mein masrat pe bari shartein hain

Sochata hoon ki mohabbat hai ek afsurda-si laash
Chaadare-izzato-namoos mein kafnaai hui
Daure-sarmaya ki raundi hui ruswa hasti
Dargahe-mazahabo-ikhlaaq se thukraai hui

Sochata hoon ki bashar aur mohabbat ka junoon
Yese bosida tamddup ye hai ek kare-zaboon

---

1. दीप्त, 2. जीवन 3. संस्कृति में 4. उदास 5. इज़्ज़त-रूपी चादर में 6. पूंजी (के आधिपत्य) के युग 7. धर्म तथा नैतिकता की दरगाह से 8. मनुष्य 9. बुरा कार्य

And it is almost impossible to wish it away
I know love has harsh pre-conditions
This culture has many pre-requisites
Covered in a coffin of respectability
Scorned by religion and morality,
Trampled and trounced by the rich and the wealthy
It entails a near death-in-life state

→

सोचता हूं कि मोहब्बत न बचेगी ज़िंदा
पेश-अज़-वक़्त कि[1] सड़ जाए ये गलती हुई लाश
यही बेहतर है कि बेगाना-ए-उल्फ़त[2] होकर
अपने सीने में करूं जज़्ब-ए-नफ़रत की[3] तलाश

और सौदा-ए-मोहब्बत[4] से किनारा कर लूं
दिल को बेगाना-ए-तरग़ीबो-तमन्ना कर लूं

Sochata hoon ki mohabbat na bachegi zinda
Pesh-az-waqt ki sad jaye ye galti hui laash
Yahi behtar hai ki begana-e-ulfat hokar
Apne sine mein karoon jazb-e-nafrat ki talaash

Aur sauda-e-mohabbat se kinara kar loon
Dil ko begana-e-targeebo-tamanna kar loon

---

1. इससे पूर्व कि 2. प्रेम से विमुख होकर 3. घृणा-भाव की 4. प्रेमोन्माद

I sometime feel that love's days are numbered
And before this dying entity starts stinking
I should engender feelings of hatred in my heart
Give up all inclination and desire for love
And thus freeing myself from this infatuation
Discard it altogether

फ़रार

अपने माज़ी के[1] तसव्वुर से[2] हिरासां[3] हूं मैं
अपने गुज़रे हुए ऐयाम से[4] नफ़रत है मुझे
अपनी बेकार तमन्नाओं पे शर्मिन्दा हूं
अपनी बेसूद[5] उमीदों पे नदामत है मुझे

मेरे माज़ी को अंधेरे में दबा रहने दो
मेरा माज़ी मेरी ज़िल्लत के सिवा कुछ भी नहीं
मेरा उमीदों का हासिल, मेरी काविश का सिला[6]
एक बेनाम अज़ीयत के[7] सिवा कुछ भी नहीं

कितनी बेकार उमीदों का सहारा लेकर
मैंने ऐवान[8] सजाए थे किसी की ख़ातिर
कितनी बेरब्त[9] तमन्नाओं के मुबहम ख़ाके[10]
अपने ख़्वाबों में बसाए थे किसी की ख़ातिर

→

Apne mazi ke tasvvur se hirasa hoon main
Apne guzare huye aeyaam se nafarat hai mujhe
Apni bekar tamannaon pe sharminda hoon
Apni besood umeedon pe nadamat hai mujhe

Mere mazi ko andhere mein daba rahno do
Mera mazi meri zillat ke siwa kuchh bhi nahin
Mera umeedon ka hasil, meri kavish ka sila
Ek benaam aziyat ke siwa kuchh bhi nahin

Kitni bekar umeedon ka sahara lekar
Maine aewan sajaye the kisi ki khatir
Kitni berabt tamannaon ke mubham khake
Apne khwabon mein basaye the kisi ki khatir

---

1. अतीत के 2. कल्पना से 3. भयभीत 4. दिनों से 5. व्यर्थ 6. प्रयत्न का फल 7. कष्ट 8. महल 9. असंगत 10. अस्पष्ट रेखाचित्र

Escapist

I feel petrified when I think of my past
I am ashamed of my dreams unrealistic
And my useless hopes

Let the gloom of my past days remain buried
My past is nothing but a humiliating tale
And a nameless misery is what I got
By way of reward for my efforts and hope

How on the silly, futile hope of making somebody my own
I had built castles in the air
How I had drawn meaningless sketches
In somebody's name

→

मुझसे अब मेरी मोहब्बत के फ़साने[1] न कहो
मुझको कहने दो कि मैंने उन्हें चाहा ही नहीं
और वो मस्त निगाहें जो मुझे भूल गईं
मैंने उन मस्त निगाहों को सराहा ही नहीं

मुझको कहने दो कि मैं आज भी जी सकता हूं
इश्क़ नाकाम सही, ज़िंदगी नाकाम नहीं
उन्हें अपनाने की ख़्वाहिश, उन्हें पाने की तलब
शौक़े-बेकार[2] सही, सअ़इ-ए-ग़म-अंजाम[3] नहीं

वही गेसू[4], वही नज़रें,वही आरिज़[5], वही जिस्म
मैं जो चाहूं तो मुझे और भी मिल सकते हैं
वो कंवल जिनको कभी उनके लिए खिलना था
उनकी नज़रों से बहुत दूर भी खिल सकते हैं

Mujhse ab meri mohabbat ke fasaane na kaho
Mujhko kahane do ki maine unhe chaha hi nahi
Aur wo mast nigahein jo mujhe bhool gain
Maine un mast nigahon ko saraha hi nahin

Mujhko kahane do ki main aaj bhi ji sakata hoon
Ishq nakaam sahi, zindgi nakaam nahin
Unhe apnane ki khwahish, unhe pane ki talab
Shauqe-bekar sahi, saai-e-gham-anjaam nahin

Wahi gesu, wahi nazarein, wahi aariz, wahi jism
Main jo chahoon to mujhe aur bhi mil sakte hain
Wo kanwal jinko kabhi unke liye khilna tha
Unki nazaron se bahut door bhi khil sakte hain

---

1. कहानियां 2. बेकार शौक़ 3. दुखांत चेष्टा 4. केश 5. कपोल

Tell me not the tales of my love
Let me say that I never loved her
And those inebriated eyes that do not recognize me
I have never admired them ever

Let me say that I can live jolly well without her
I may be a failure in love but not a failure in life really
The desire to win her for my own may have remained unfulfilled
But it is not a tragedy

If I wish I can get elsewhere too
Curls and cheeks, eyes and the rest like hers
And the lotus flowers which had once to blossom for her
I can make them blossom far away from her eyes too

इसी दोराहे पर!

अब न इन ऊंचे मकानों में क़दम रखूंगा
मैंने इक बार ये पहले भी क़सम खाई थी
अपनी नादार मोहब्बत की शिकस्तों के तुफ़ैल
ज़िंदगी पहले भी शर्माई थी, झुंझलाई थी

और ये अ़हद[1] किया था कि ब-ईं-हाले-तबाह[2]
अब कभी प्यार भरे गीत नहीं गाऊंगा
किसी चिलमन ने पुकारा भी तो बढ़ जाऊंगा
कोई दरवाज़ा खुला भी तो पलट आऊंगा

फिर तेरे कांपते होंटों की फ़ुसूंकार[3] हंसी
जाल बुनने लगी, बुनती रही, बुनती ही रही
मैं खिंचा तुझसे, मगर तू मेरी राहों के लिए
फूल चुनती रही, चुनती रही, चुनती ही रही

→

Ab na in unche makanon mein kadam rakhunga
Maine ek baar ye pahle bhi kasam khai thi
Apni nadar mohabbat ki shikaston ke tufail
Zindgi pahle bhi sharmai thi, jhunjhalai thi

Aur ye ahad kiya tha ki b-een-hale-tabaah
Ab kabhi pyaar bhare geet nahin gaunga
Kisi chilman ne pukara bhi to bad jaunga
Koi darwaza khula bhi to palat aaunga

Phir tere kaanpte honton ki phusoonkar hansi
Jaal bunne lagi, bunti rahi, bunti hi rahi
Main khincha tujhse, magar tu meri raahon ke liye
Phool chunti rahi, chunti rahi, chunti hi rahi

---

1. प्रतिज्ञा 2. तबाह-हाल होने पर भी 3. जादू-भरी

On the same crossroads

Earlier too I had sworn once
That I will never enter these buildings tall
Earlier too because of my failure in love
I had felt ashamed and cursed myself

I had resolved that even in the worst of circumstances
I will never write love songs again
Even if some beauty beckons me, even if some door
for me opens
I will care not and move on

And then your bewitching smile
Began laying snares and went on laying them
I withheld myself but you began to strew flowers on
my way
And went on strewing them

→

बर्फ़ बरसाई मेरे ज़ेहनो-तसव्वुर ने[1] मगर
दिल में इक शो'लाए-बेनाम-सा[2] लहरा ही गया
तेरी चुपचाप निगाहों को सुलगते पाकर
मेरी बेज़ार तबीयत को भी प्यार आ ही गया

अपनी बदली हुई नज़रों के तक़ाज़े न छुपा
मैं इस अन्दाज़ का मफ़हूम[3] समझ सकता हूं
तेरे ज़रकार[4] दरीचों की बुलन्दी की क़सम
अपने अक़दाम का मक़सूम[5] समझ सकता हूं

'अब न इन ऊंचे मकानों में क़दम रखूंगा'
मैंने इक बार ये पहले भी क़सम खाई थी
इसी सर्माया-ओ इफ़्लास के दोराहे पर
ज़िंदगी पहले भी शर्माई थी, झुंझलाई थी

Barf barsaai mere zehano-tasvvur ne magar
Dil mein ek sho-laye-benaam-sa lahara hi gaya
Teri chupchaap nigahon ko sulgate pakar
Meri bezar tabiyat ko bhi pyaar aa hi gaya

Apni badli hui nazaron ke taqaze na chupaa
Main is andaaz ka mafhoom samajh sakta hoon
Tere zarkaar darichon ki bulandi ki kasam
Apne aqdaam ka maqsoom samajh sakata hoon

'Ab na in unche makanon mein kadam rakhoonga
Maine ek baar ye pahle bhi kasam khai thi
Isi sarmaya-o iflaas ke dorahe par
Zindgi pahle bhi sharmai thi, jhunjhalai thi

---

1. मस्तिष्क तथा कल्पना ने 2. बेनाम-सा शो'ला 3. अर्थ 4. स्वर्णिम 5. क़दम उठाने का भाग्य

My mind revolted but in my heart
A nameless flame began to rise
When I saw your burning lips
In spite of my misery, I couldn't help loving you

Hide not the reasons behind your changed attitude
I can understand the motive for this change
I swear by you casements golden and grand
I can understand the meaning of your action

I will never enter these tall buildings again
Earlier too I had sworn once
On the crossroads of riches and poverty
Once earlier too I had felt ashamed and cursed myself

एक तस्वीरे-रंग

मैंने जिस वक़्त तुझे पहले-पहल देखा था
तू जवानी का कोई ख़्वाब नज़र आई थी
हुस्न का नग़्मए-जावेद[1] हुई थी मालूम
इश्क़ का जज़्बाए-बेताब[2] नज़र आई थी

ऐ तरबज़ारे-जवानी[3] की परेशां तितली
तू भी इक बूए-गिरफ़्तार[4] है, मालूम न था
तेरे जल्वों में बहारें नज़र आई थीं मुझे
तू सितम-ख़ुर्दहे-अदबार[5] है, मालूम न था

तेरे नाज़ुक से परों पर ये ज़रो-सीम का[6] बोझ
तेरी परवाज़[7] को आज़ाद न होने देगा
तूने राहत की तमन्ना में जो ग़म पाला है
वो तेरी रूह को आबाद न होने देगा

→

Maine jis waqt tujhe pahle-pahal dekha tha
Tu jawani ka koi khwab nazar aai thi
Husn ka nagmaye-jawed hui thi maloom
Ishq ka jazbaye-betaab nazar aai thi

Ye tarbazare-jawani ki pareshan titli
Tu bhi ek booy-giraftaar hai, maloom na tha
Tere jalwo mein baharein nazar aai thin mujhe
Tu sitam-khurd he-adbaar hai, maloom na tha

Tere nazuk se paron par ye zaro-seem ka bojh
Teri parwaz ko aazad na hone dega
Tune rahat ki tamanna mein jo gham pala hai
Wo teri rooh ko aabad na hone dega

---

1. अनन्त संगीत 2. विकल भावना 3. यौवन-रूपी उद्यान 4. बन्दी सुगन्ध 5. दुर्भाग्य के हाथों पीड़ित 6. सोने-चांदी का 7. उड़ान

A picture of colours

When I saw you for the first time
You appeared to be a dream of youth
Appeared to be an eternal song of beauty
Felt like a haunting passion of love

O butterfly of the garden of youth
I didn't know that you yourself were a fragrance, imprisoned
Your beauty was a picture of spring
You were stricken by a calamity I did not know

The weight of gold and silver on your delicate wings
Will not let you freely fly
And the sufferings you bear in the hope of future comfort
Will not let your heart know any peace

→

तूने सर्माए की छाओं में पनपने के लिए
अपने दिल, अपनी मोहब्बत का लहू बेचा है
दिन की तज़ुईने-फ़ुसुर्दा[1] का असासा[2] लेकर
रात की शोख़ मसर्रत का लहू बेचा है

इससे क्या फ़ायदा रंगीन लबादों के[3] तले
रूह जलती रहे, गलती रहे, पज़मुर्दा[4] रहे
होंट हंसते हों दिखावे के तबस्सुम[5] के लिए
दिल ग़मे-ज़ीस्त[6] से बोझिल रहे आज़ुर्दा[7] रहे

दिल की तस्कीं[8] भी है आसाइशे-हस्ती[9] की दलील
ज़िंदगी सिर्फ़ ज़रो-सीम का[10] पैमाना नहीं
ज़ीस्त एहसास[11] भी है, शौक़ भी है, दर्द भी है
सिर्फ़ अन्फ़ास[12] की तरतीब का अफ़साना नहीं

→

Tune sarmaye ki chhaaon mein panpane ke liye
Apne dil, apni mohabbat ka lahoo becha hai
Din ki tazuine-fusuda ka asasa lekar
Raat ki shokh masrrat ka lahoo becha hai

Isse kya fayada rangeen labadon ke tale
Rooh jalti rahe, galti rahe, pazmurda rahe
Hont hanste hon dikhawe ke tabssum ke liye
Dil ghame-zist se bojhil rahe aazurda rahe

Dil ki taskin bhi hai aasaishe-hasti ki dalil
Zindgi sirf zaro-seem ka paimana nahin
Zist ahsaas bhi hai, shauq bhi hai, dard bhi hai
Sirf anfaas ki tarteeb ka afsana nahin

---

1. रूखी-फीकी सज्जा 2. निधि 3. वस्त्रों के 4. मुर्झाई हुई 5. मुस्कान 6. जीवन के ग़म 7. चिन्तित 8. संतोष 9. जीवन के सुख 10. चांदी-सोने का 11. अनुभूति 12. श्वासों की

In order to live in the midst of riches
You have murdered your love, sold your heart
And for the sake of dull decorations of daytime
Sacrificed the joys of your nights

What is the worth of your life under the gaudy dresses
Your spirits are whittled and become lifeless
Or if you keep smiling an artificial smile
While your life becomes a dull burdensome affair

The projected comforts of life seem to please you at this moment
But life is not just gold and silver
It is not merely the number of breaths you breathe
Life is feelings, life is love, life is pain too

→

उम्र भर रेंगते रहने से कहीं बेहतर है
एक लम्हा जो तेरी रूह में वुस'अत[1] भर दे
एक लम्हा जो तेरे गीत को शोख़ी दे दे
एक लम्हा जो तेरी लै में मसर्रत भर दे

Umr bhar rengte rahne se kahin behatar hai
Ek lamha jo teri rooh mein vusat bhar de
Ek lamha jo tere geet ko shokhi de de
Ek lamha jo teri lai mein masrrat bhar de

---

1. विशालता

A moment that lends you width and flight
A moment that gives you a joyous song
And fills the rhythm of life, with happiness
Is any day better than a life-long crawling

मा'ज़ूरी[1]

ख़ल्वतो-जल्वत में[2] तुम मुझसे मिली हो बारहा
तुमने क्या देखा नहीं, मैं मुस्करा सकता नहीं
मैं कि मायूसी मेरी फ़ितरत में[3] दाख़िल हो चुकी
जब्र भी ख़ुद पर करूं तो गुनगुना सकता नहीं

मुझमें क्या देखा कि तुम उल्फ़त का दम भरने लगीं
मैं तो खुद अपने भी कोई काम आ सकता नहीं
रूह-अफ़ज़ा[4] हैं जूनूने-इश्क़ के[5] नग़्मे मगर
अब मैं इन गाए हुए गीतों को गा सकता नहीं

मैंने देखा है शिकस्ते-साज़े-उल्फ़त का समां[6]
अब किसी तहरीक पर[7] बरबत[8] उठा सकता नहीं
दिल तुम्हारी शिद्दते-एहसास[9] से वाक़िफ़ तो है,
अपने अहसासात से दामन छुड़ा सकता नहीं

→

Khalwato-jalwat mein tum mujhse mili ho barha
Tumne kya dekha nahin, main muskara sakta hoon
Main ki mayoosi meri fitrat mein dakhil ho chuki
Jabr bhi khud par karoon to gunguna sakta nahin

Mujhmein kya dekha ki tum ulfat ka dam bharne lagin
Main to khud apne bhi koi kaam aa sakta nahin
Rooh-afaza hain junune-ishq ke nagme magar
Ab main in gaye huye geeton ko ga sakta nahin

Maine dekha hai shikaste-saaze-ulfat ka samaa
Ab kisi tahreek par barbat utha sakta nahin
Dil tumhari shiddate-ahsaas se waqif to hai,
Apne ahsaasat se daman chhuda sakta nahin

---

1. विवशता 2. एकांत में और सबके सामने 3. स्वभाव में 4. प्राणवर्धक 5. प्रेमोन्माद के 6. प्रेम-रूपी साज़ के टूटने का दृश्य 7. प्रेरणा पर 8. एक बाजा 9. अनुभूति की तीव्रता

Helplessness

You have often seen me alone as well as in public
Have you not noticed that till date I cannot smile
Despair has so much seeped into my heart
That I cannot hum a song however much I try

What did you see in me that you started loving me
I am of no use even to myself
The songs of love are life-enhancing though
Even those songs which I had sung earlier, I can no longer sing

I have seen the musical instrument that played songs of love crashing, and now
Nothing can inspire me to play on any instrument
I know the intensity of your feelings though
I cannot overcome my own feelings

→

तुम मेरी होकर भी बेगाना ही पाओगी मुझे
मैं तुम्हारा होके भी तुम में समा सकता नहीं
गाए हैं मैंने ख़लूसे दिल से[1] *भी उल्फ़त के गीत*
अब रियाकारी से भी चाहूं तो गा सकता नहीं

किस तरह तुमको बना लूं मैं शरीके-ज़िंदगी[2]
मैं तो अपनी ज़िंदगी का बार[3] *उठा सकता नहीं*
यास की[4] *तारीकियों में*[5] *डूब जाने दो मुझे*
अब मैं शमए-आरज़ू की[6] *लौ बढ़ा सकता नहीं*

Tum meri hokar bhi begana hi paaogi mujhe
Main tumhara hoke bhi tum mein samaa sakta nahin
Gaye hain maine khaloose dil se bhi ulfat ke geet
Ab riyakari se bhi chahon to ga sakta nahin

Kis tarah tumko bana loon main shareeke-zindgi
Main to apni zindgi ka baar utha sakta nahin
Yaas ki tareekiyon mein doob jane do mujhe
Ab main shamye-aarzoo ki lau bada sakta nahi

---

1. शुद्ध-हृदयता से 2. जीवन-साथी 3. बोझ 4. निराशा की 5. अंधेरों में 6. कामनारूपी दीपक की

You are mine and still you will find me to be a stranger
I belong to you and yet I cannot be part of you
The love songs that I have sung from the core of my heart
Even out of expediency, I cannot sing them now

How can I make you my life-partner
I cannot look after myself either
Let me be lost in the darkness of despair
For I no longer can afford to harbour any desire

.ख़ुदकुशी से पहले

उफ़ ये बेदर्द सियाही ये हवा के नौहे[1]
किसको मालूम है इस शब की[2] सहर[3] हो कि न हो
इक नज़र तेरे दरीचे की तरफ़ देख तो लूं
डूबती आंखों में फ़िर ताबे-नज़र[4] हो कि न हो

अभी रौशन हैं तेरे गर्म शबिस्तां के[5] दिये
नीलगूं पर्दों से छनती हैं शुआयें अब तक
अजनबी बांहों के हल्क़े में लचकती होंगी
तेरे महके हुए बालों की रिदायें[6] अब तक

सर्द होती हुई बत्ती के धुएं के हमराज़
हाथ फैलाए बढ़े आते हैं बोझिल साए
कौन पोंछे मेरी आंखों के सुलगते आंसू
कौन उलझे हुए बालों की गिरह सुलझाए

→

Uf ye bedard siyahi ye hawa ke nauhe
Kisko maloom hai is shab ki sahar ho ki na ho
Ek nazar tere dariche ki taraf dekh to loon
Doobti aankhon mein phir taabe-nazar ho ki na ho

Abhi roshan hain tere garm shabistan ke diye
Neelgoon pardon se chhanti hain shuaayen ab tak
Ajnabi baanhon ke halke mein lachkati hongi
Tere mahake huye baalon ki ridayein ab tak

Sard hoti hui batti ke dhuyein ke hamraj
Hath phailaye bade aate hain bojhil saaye
Kaun ponchhe meri aankon ke sulagte aansoo
Kaun uljhe huye baalon ki girah suljhaye

---

1. विलाप 2. रात की 3. सुबह 4. देखने की शक्ति 5. शयनागार के 6. चादरें, लटें

Before the suicide

Ah this murderous darkness, this dirge in the wind
This night may or may not end
Let me cast a last glance at your window
For, my sinking eyes may not have sight in them for long

Lights in your bedroom are still on
Their beams are still coming through the blue curtains
O your rich fragrant hair must still be falling on the stranger's arms

Alongwith the smoke from dimming lights
Thick black shadows are embracing the night
Who will wipe the scalding tears from my eyes
And clean out the dust from my disheveled hair

→

आह ये ग़ारे-हलाक़त[1], ये दिये का महबस[2]
उम्र अपनी इन्हीं तारीक[3] मकानों में कटी
ज़िंदगी फ़ितरते-बेहिस की[4] पुरानी तक़सीर[5]
इक हक़ीक़त[6] थी मगर चंद फ़सानों में कटी

कितनी आसाइशें[7] हंसती रहीं ऐवानों में[8]
कितने दर[9] मेरी जवानी पे सदा बन्द रहे
कितने हाथों ने बुना अतलसो-कमख़्वाब मगर
मेरे मलबूस की[10] तक़दीर में पेबन्द रहे

ज़ुल्म सहते हुए इन्सानों के इस मक़तल[11] में
कोई फ़र्दा के[12] तसव्वुर से कहां तक बहले
उम्र भर रेंगते रहने की सज़ा है जीना
एक-दो दिन की अज़ीयत[13] हो तो कोई सह ले

→

Aah ye gaare-halaaqat, ye diye ka mahbas
Umr apni inhin tareekh makanon mein kati
Zindgi fitrate-behis ki purani taqseer
Ek haqiqat thi magar chand fasane mein kati

Kitni aasaishe hansti rahin aewanon mein
Kitne dar meri jawani pe sada band rahe
Kitne hathon ne buna atlaso-kamkhwab magar
Mere malboos ki taqdeer mein peband rahe

Zulm sahte huye insaanon ke is maqtal mein
Koi farda ke tasvvur se kahan tak bahle
Umr bhar rengte rahne ki saza hai jeena
Ek-do din ki aziyat ho to koi sah le

---

1. विनाश की कन्दरा 2. कारावास 3. अंधेरे 4. निष्ठुर प्रकृति की 5. अपराध 6. वास्तविकता 7. सुख-समृद्धियां 8. महलों में, 9. दरवाज़े 10. लिबास की 11. वध-स्थल 12. आने वाले कल के 13. दुःख

O the caverns of death where light is forbidden
We have passed all our life in these dark houses
It was but a punishment from cruel nature

So many living in luxurious houses laughed at me
So many doors were slammed on my youth
So many hands wove fine linens though
My apparel was destined to be covered with patches

In this slaughter house for people groaning under tyranny
How can we live in the hope of a bright tomorrow?
Suffering for a day or two one can easily bear
But here crawling all his life is the lot of man

→

वही ज़ुल्मत[1] है फ़ज़ाओं पे[2] अभी तक तारी
जाने कब ख़त्म हो इन्सां के लहू की तक़तीर[3]
जाने कब निखरे सियहपोश फ़ज़ा का[4] जोबन
जाने कब जागे सितम-ख़ुर्दा बशर की[5] तक़दीर

अभी रौशन हैं तेरे गर्म शबिस्तां के दीये
आज मैं मौत के ग़ारों में उतर जाऊंगा
और दम तोड़ती बत्ती के धुएं के हमराह
सरहदे-मर्गे-मुसलसल से[6] गुज़र जाऊंगा

Wahi zulmat hai fizaaon pe abhi tak tari
Jane kab khatm ho insaan ke lahoo ki taqdir
Jane kab nikhare siyahposh faza ka joban
Jane kab jaage sitam-khurda bashar ki taqdir

Abhi roshan hain tere garm shabistan ke diye
Aaj main maut ke gharon mein utar jaoonga
Aur dam todti batti ke dhuyein ke hamraah
Sarhade-magen-musalsal se guzar jaoonga

---

1. अंधेरा 2. वातावरण पर 3. बूंद-बूंद टपकना 4. काले वातावरण का 5. अत्याचार-पीड़ित मनुष्य की 6. निरन्तर मृत्यु की सीमा से

Ancient darkness still covers the atmosphere
Nobody knows when this dripping of human blood will
stop
When the boom of this darkness will burst
Nobody knows when the fortunes of oppressed
humanity will change

Lights in your cosy bedroom are still on
Today I will descend in the caverns of death
And alongside the smoke from dimming light
beyond the realms of slow death
I will break away from daily death-in-life

नूरजहां के मज़ार पर

पहलुए-शाह में[1] ये दुख़्तरे-जमहूर की[2] क़ब्र
कितने गुमगश्ता फ़सानों का[3] पता देती है
कितने ख़ूरेज़ हक़ायक़ से[4] उठाती है नक़ाब
कितनी कुचली हुई जानों का पता देती है
कैसे मग़रूर शहनशाहों की तस्कीं के लिए
सालहासाल हसीनाओं के बाज़ार लगे
कैसे बहकी हुई नज़रों के तअय्युश[5] के लिए
सुर्ख़ महलों में जवां जिस्मों के अंबार लगे
कैसे हर शाख़ से मुंह-बंद महकती कलियां
नोच ली जाती थीं तज़ईने-हरम[6] की ख़ातिर
और मुर्झा के भी आज़ाद न हो सकती थीं
ज़िल्ले-सुबहान की[7] उलफ़त के भरम की ख़ातिर

→

Pahluye-shaah mein ye dukhtare-jamhoor ki kabr
Kitne gumgashta fasanon ka pataa deti hai
Kitne khoonrej haqayaq se uthati hai naqab
Kitni kuchli hui janon ka pataa deti hai
Kaise maghroor shahanshaahon ki taskin ke liye
Saalhasaal hasinaon ke bazar lage
Kaise bahaki hui nazaron ke taayyush ke liye
Surkh mahalon mein jawan jismon ke ambaar lage
Kaise har shaakh se munh-band mahakti
Noch li jati thin tazaine-haram ki khatir
Aur murjha ke bhi aazad na ho sakti thi
Zille-subhaan ki ulfat ke bharam ki khatir

---

1. बादशाह की बग़ल में 2. जनता की बेटी की 3. भूली-बिसरी कहानियों का 4. रक्तिम वास्तविकताओं से 5. विलास-प्रियता 6. हरम की शोभा 7. बादशाह की

At Noorjahan's tomb

This grave of democracy beside the emperor's tomb
Holds a key to many an unknown tale
Unveils so much blood-stained reality
And gives a clue to numberless lives trampled over,
It tells us how to entertain an overbearing emperor
Beauties were paraded in the market place,
How in order to gratify his lustful eyes
Red palaces would teem with youthful maidens
How in order to enhance the grandeur of his *heram*
Unblossomed buds were plucked from every bough
And under the illusion that they enjoyed the emperor's favour
They could not free themselves even when they had withered away

→

कैसे इक फ़र्द के[1] होंटों की ज़रा-सी जुंबिश
सर्द कर सकती थी बेलौस[2] वफ़ाओं के चिराग़
लूट सकती थी दमकते हुए हाथों का सुहाग
तोड़ सकती थी मए-इश्क़ से[3] लबरेज़ अयाग़[4]
सहमी-सहमी-सी फ़ज़ाओं में ये वीरां मरक़द[5]
इतना ख़ामोश है, फ़रियाद-कुनां[6] हो जैसे
सर्द शाखों में हवा चीख़ रही है ऐसे
रूहे-तक़दीसो-वफ़ा[7] मर्सियाख़्वां हो[8] जैसे
तू मेरी जान! मुझे हैरतो-हसरत से न देख
हम में कोई भी जहांनूरो-जहांगीर नहीं
तू मुझे छोड़ के ठुकरा के भी जा सकती है
तेरे हाथों में मेरे हाथ हैं, ज़ंजीर नहीं

Kaise ek fard ke honton ki zara-si jumbish
Sard kar sakti thi belaus wafaaon ke chiraag
Loot sakti thi damkte huye hathon ka suhaag
Tod sakti thi mye-ishq se labrez ayaag
Sahmi-Sahmi-si fazaaon mein ye viraan marqad
Itna khamosh hai, fariyaad-kuna ho jaise
Sard shaakhon mein hawa chikh rahi hai yese
Roohe-taqdiso-wafa marsiyakhwan ho jaise
Tu meri jaan! mujhe hairato-hasrat se na dekh
Hum mein koi bhi jahanooro-jahangir nahin
Tu mujhe chhod ke thukra ke bhi ja sakti hai
Tere hathon mein mere hath hain, janzeer nahin

---

1. व्यक्ति के 2. निष्काम 3. प्रेम-रूपी मदिरा से 4. भरे हुए प्याले 5. क़ब्र 6. न्याय की दुहाई दे रहा 7. प्रेम तथा पवित्रता की आत्मा 8. विलाप कर रही हो

How just a wink from the emperor
Could blow out the light of boundless love
How it could widow a flashing bride
And break the goblet with love overflowing
In this heavy atmosphere Noorjahan's desolate tomb
Is so quiet as if it were crying for justice
And the wind is howling through cold branches
As if the spirit of love and piety were singing a dirge

My love, do not look at me with suspicion and longing
Nobody among us is either a Jahangir or Noorjahan
You can reject and leave me if you so desire
I can never forcibly hold you my dear

मेरे गीत

मेरे सरकश[1] तराने सुनके दुनिया ये समझती है
कि शायद मेरे दिल को इश्क़ के नग़्मों से नफ़रत है

मुझे हंगामा-ए-जंगो-जदल[2] में कैफ़[3] मिलता है
मेरी फ़ितरत[4] को ख़ूरेज़ी[5] के अफ़सानों से रग़बत[6] है

मेरी दुनिया में कुछ वक़्अत[7] नहीं है रक़्सो-नग़्मे की[8]
मेरा महबूब नग़्मां[9] शोरे-आहंगे-बग़ावत है

मगर ऐ काश! देखें वो मेरी पुरसोज़[10] रातों को
मैं जब तारों प नज़रें गाड़कर आंसू बहाता हूं

तसव्वुर[11] बनके भूली वारदातें[12] याद आती हैं
तो सोज़ो-दर्द की शिद्दत[13] से पहरों तिलमिलाता हूं

→

Mere sarkash tarane sunke duniya ye samjhti hai
Ki shaayad mere dil ko ishq ke nagmon se nafrat hai

Mujhe hangama-e-jango-jadal mein kaif milta hai
Meri fitrat ko khoonrezi ke afsaanon se ragbat hai

Meri duniya mein kuchh waqat nahin hai raqso-nagme ki
Mera mahboob nagma shore-aahange-baghaawat hai

Magar ye kaash! dekhen vo meri pursoz raaton ko
Main jab taaron pe nazarein gaadkar aansu bahaata hoon

Tasvvur banke bhooli wardatein yaad aati hain
To sozo-dard ki shiddat se paharon tilmilata hoon

---

1. विद्रोहपूर्ण 2. युद्ध और संघर्ष 3. आनन्द 4. स्वभाव 5. ख़ून बहाना 6. रुचि 7. मूल्य 8. नृत्य और संगीत की 9. प्रिय संगीत 10. दर्द भरी 11. कल्पना 12. घटनाएं, 13. तीव्रता

My songs

Listening to my rebellious songs, people say
That I hate the songs of love, it looks
That I enjoy the tumult of war and struggle
Love the tales of bloodshed

Love the loud calls for rebellion
And care not for dance and music
How I wish they were a witness to my painful nights
When with my eyes fixed on the stars, I cry

When the tragedies of the past flash upon my mind
And in anguish, I sigh

→

कोई ख़्वाबों में ख़्वाबीदा[1] उमंगों को जगाती है
तो अपनी ज़िंदगी को मौत के पहलू में पाता हूं

मैं शायर हूं मुझे फ़ितरत[2] के नज़ारों से उल्फ़त है
मेरा दिल दुश्मने-नग़्मा-सराई[3] हो नहीं सकता

मुझे इन्सानियत का दर्द भी बख़्शा है क़ुदरत ने
मेरा मक़सद फ़क़त[4] शोला-नवाई[5] हो नहीं सकता

जवां हूं मैं जवानी लग़्ज़िशों का[6] एक तूफ़ां है
मेरी बातों में रंगे-पारसाई[7] हो नहीं सकता

मेरे सरकश तरानों की हक़ीक़त[8] है तो इतनी है
कि जब मैं देखता हूं भूख के मारे किसानों को

→

Koi khwabon mein khwabeeda umangon ko jagaati hai
To apni zindgi ko maut ke pahloo mein pata hoon

Mein shaayar hoon mujhe fitrat ke nazzaron se ulfat hai
Mera dil dushmane-nagma-saraai ho nahin sakta

Mujhe insaaniyat ka dard bhi bakhsha hai qudrat ne
Mera maqsad faqat shola-nawai ho nahin sakta

Jawan hoon main jawani lagzishon ka ek toofan hai
Meri baton mein range-paarsai ho nahin sakta

Mere sarkash taranon ki haqiqat hai to itni hai
Ki jab main dekhta hoon bhookh ke mare kisanon ko

---

1. सोई हुई 2. प्रकृति 3. गीत गाने का विरोधी 4. केवल 5. आग बरसाना 6. लड़खड़ाहटों का
7. पवित्रता का रंग 8. वास्तविकता

When a certain damsel awakes my desires and dream,
long buried
And I feel that I will die

I am a poet and I love natural beauty
I can never be hostile to song and music
But I felt most acutely the sufferings of humanity
And merely spewing fire is not my purpose

I am a young man and youth is an age of romance
I can never smack of unnecessary piety.
But when I see the starving peasantry,
Impoverished and helpless humanity

→

ग़रीबों, मुफ़लिसों को, बेकसों को, बेसहारों को
सिसकती नाज़नीनों को, तड़पते नौजवानों को

हुकूमत के तशद्दुद[1] को, अमारत[2] के तकब्बुर[3] को
किसी के चीथड़ों को और शहनशाही खज़ानों को

तो दिल ताबे-निशाते-बज़्मे-इश्रत ला नहीं सकता[4]
मैं चाहूं भी तो ख़्वाब-आवर[5] तराने गा नहीं सकता

Garibon, muflison ko, bekason ko, besaharon ko
Sisakti nazaninon ko, tadpte naujawanon ko

Hukoomat ke tashaddud ko, amaarat ke takbbur ko
Kisi ke chithadon ko aur shahanshahi khazanon ko

To dil taabe-nishate-bazme-ishrat la nahin sakta
Main chahoon bhi to khwab-aavar tarane gaa nahin sakta

---

1. हिंसा 2. धन-दौलत 3. घमण्ड 4. वैभवपूर्ण समाज के ऐश्वर्य को सहन नहीं कर सकता
5. सुलाने वाले

When I see sobbing maidens and smarting young men
When I see the arrogance of the rulers and insolence
of the rich
When I see the people in rags on one side
And regal splendour on the other

Then I cannot reconcile to this vulgar display of wealth
And just cannot sing soothing song of love

कल और आज

कल भी बूंदें बरसी थीं
कल भी बादल छाए थे
और कवि ने सोचा था!

बादल ये आकाश के सपने इन ज़ुल्फ़ों के साए हैं
दोशे-हवा पर[1] मैख़ाने ही मैख़ाने घिर आए हैं
रुत बदलेगी फूल खिलेंगे झोंके मधु बरसाएंगे
उजले-उजले खेतों में रंगीं आंचल लहराएंगे
चरवाहें बंसी की धुन से गीत फ़ज़ा में बोएंगे
आमों के झुण्डों के नीचे परदेसी दिल खोलेंगे
पेंग बढ़ाती गोरी के माथे से कौंदे लपकेंगे
जोहड़ के ठहरे पानी में तारे आंखें झपकेंगे

→

Kal bhi boondein barasi thin
Kal bhi badal chhaye the
Aur kavi ne socha tha!

Baadal ye aakash ke sapne in zulfon ke saaye hain
doshe-hawa par maikhane hi maikhane ghir aaye hain
Rut badlegi phool khilenge jhonke madhu barsayenge
Ujle-ujle kheton mein rangin aanchal lahrayenge
Charwahe bansi ki dhun se geet faza mein boyenge
Aamon ke jhundon ke niche pardesi dil kholenge
Peng badati gori ke mathe se kaunde lapkenge
Johar ke thahre paani mein taare aankhen jhapkenge

1. वायु के कन्धे पर

Yesterday and today

The sky was overcast yesterday too
Yesterday too the raindrops fell
And the poet imagined:
These clouds, the dream of heavens are but a shade
of her tresses
Taverns upon taverns are floating on the wind
Now the weather will change, flowers blossom and
manna dew will rain
And in the lush green fields beautiful damsels dance
The shepherds will sing the weather on their flute,
The travellers will pour their hearts under the mango
groves
And the fruits on the trees will scramble to kiss the
maidens up on the swing
And the stars will twinkle on the stationary pool

→

उलझी-उलझी राहों में वो आंचल थामे आएंगे
धरती, फूल, आकाश, सितारे सपना-सा बन जाएंगे
कल भी बूंदे बरसी थीं
कल भी बादल छाए थे
और कवि ने सोचा था!

आज भी बूंदें बरसेंगी
आज भी बादल छाए हैं
और कवि इस सोच में है!
बस्ती पर बादल छाए हैं, पर ये बस्ती किसकी है
धरती पर अमृत बरसेगा, लेकिन धरती किसकी है
हल जोतेगी खेतों में अल्हड़ टोली दहक़ानों की[1]
धरती से फूटेगी मेहनत फ़ाक़ाकश इन्सानों की

→

Uljhi-uljhi raahon mein wo aanchal thame aayenge
Dharti, phool, aakash, sitare sapna-sa ban jayenge

Kal bhi boondein barsi thin
Kal bhi baadal chhaye the
Aur kavi ne socha tha!

Aaj bhi boondein barsengi
Aaj bhi baadal chhaye hain
Aur kavi is socha mein hai!
Basti par baadal chhaye hain, par ye basti kiski hai
Dharti par amrit barsega, lekin dharti kiski hai
Hal jotegi kheton mein alhar toli insaanon ki

---

1. किसानों की

The sky, and the flower-like stars as they visit the
earth's zigzag ways
Will create a wonderland
Thus the poet sang
Yesterday too the raindrops fell
The sky was overcast yesterday too

Today also the sky will be overcast
Today also the raindrops will fall
And the poet will be lost in thought
The town is covered with clouds but whose town is it
Nectar will rain on the earth but who owns the earth
Tomorrow the fields will be ploughed by the bubbling
youthful farmers

→

फ़सलें काट के मेहनतकश, ग़ल्ले के ढेर लगाएंगे
जागीरों के मालिक आकर सब 'पूंजी' ले जाएंगे
बूढ़े दहक़ानों के घर बनिये की क़ुर्क़ी आएगी
और क़र्ज़े के सूद में कोई गोरी बेची जाएगी
आज भी जनता भूखी है और कल भी जनता तरसी थी
आज भी रिमझिम बरखा होगी, कल भी बारिश बरसी थी
आज भी बादल छाए हैं
आज भी बूंदें बरसेंगी
और कवि इस सोच में है!

Fasalein kaat ke mehnatkash, galle ke ther lagayenge
Jageeron ke maalik aakar sab poonji le jayenge
Boode dahkanon ke ghar baniye ki kurqi aayegi
Aur karze ke sood mein koi gori bechi jayegi
Aaj bhi janta bhookhi hai aur kal bhi janta tarsi thi
Aaj bhi rimjhim barkha hogi, kal bhi baarish barsi thi
Aaj bhi baadal chhaye hain
Aaj bhi boondein barsengi
Aur kavi is soch mein hai!

And the labour of starving masses will flower forth
The peasants will reap the crops and there will be heaps of grain all around
And landlords will come and gobble up the entire proceeds
The houses of the old farmers will be confiscated
And youthful maidens will be given away by way of interest payments
Today the masses are starving, tomorrow too they will starve
Today the rain will fall in streets tomorrow also it will fall
Today also the sky is overcast
Tomorrow also it will rain
And the poet will be lost in thoughts again

अब आएं या न आएं

अब आएं या न आएं इधर, पूछते चलो
क्या चाहती है उनकी नज़र पूछते चलो

हम से अगर है तर्के-तअल्लुक़[1], तो क्या हुआ
यारो! कोई तो उनकी ख़बर पूछते चलो

जो खुद को कह रहे हैं कि मंज़िल-शनास[2] हैं
उनको भी क्या ख़बर है, मगर पूछते चलो

किस मंज़िले-मुराद की जानिब रवां[3] हैं हम
ऐ रहरवाने-ख़ाक-ब-सर[4], पूछते चलो

Ab aayein ya na aayein idhar, poochhate chalo
Kya chahti hai unki nazar poochhte chalo

Hum se agar hai tarke-taalluk, to kya huaa
Yaaron! koi to unki khabar poochhte chalo

Jo khud ko kah rahe hain ki manzil-shanaas hain
Unko bhi kya khabar hai, magar poochhte chalo

Kis manzile-muraad ki janib rawaa hain hum
Ye raharwaane-khaak-b-sar, poochhte chalo

---

1. सम्बन्ध-विच्छेद 2. मंज़िल के जानकार 3. गतिशील 4. ऐसा राही जिसका सिर धूल भरा हो

We may not come here again

We may or may not pass this way again, let's find out,
What is it they are looking for, let's find out

So what, if we have in this relationship with each other
fallen out,
But friends, one of you must about his well-being find
out,

They think they know the destination,
They may or may not know, but even then find out

To which cherished destination we are proceeding
O, dust-smeared travellers find out

हर क़दम

हर क़दम हर मरहला दारो-सलीब आज भी है
जो कभी था वही इंसां का नसीब आज भी है

जगमगाए हैं उफ़क़[1] पार सितारे लेकिन
रास्ता मंज़िले-हस्ती का मुहीब[2] आज भी है

अहले-दानिश[3] ने जिसे अमरे-मुसल्लम माना
अहले-दिल के लिए वो बात अजीब आज भी है

ये तेरी ज़ात है या मेरी अज़ीयत कोशी
एक नश्तर-सा रगे-जा के क़रीब आज भी है

कौन जाने ये तेरा शायरे-आशुफ़ता-मिज़ाज[4]
कितने मग़रूर ख़ुदाओं का रक़ीब आज भी है

Har kadam har marhalaa daro-salib aaj bhi hai
Jo kabhi tha wahi insaan ka nasib aaj bhi hai

Jagmagaye hain ufaq paar sitare lekin
Rasta manzile-hasti ka muheeb aaj bhi hai

Ahle-danish ne jise amre-musallam mana
Ahle-dil ke liye wo baat ajeeb aaj bhi hai

Ye teri jaat hai ya meri aziyat koshi
Ek nastar-sa rage-ja ke karib aaj bhi hai

Kaun jane ye tera shaayare-aashufata-mizaj
Kitne magroor khudaaon ka rakeeb aaj bhi hai

---

1. क्षितिज 2. धुंधला 3. अक़्लमंद लोग 4. नाज़ुक मिज़ाज

At every step

At every step, the cross and the gallows await even today
As it was in the past, this is man's fate even today

Though beyond the horizon even today the stars are shining brightly
The way to life's destination continues to be dim and hazy

Something that the man of intellect took as final command
The man of feelings still doesn't quite understand

Is it your memory or because of my misery
Till today, a sharp knife pierces my heart from a close proximity

Who knows how many arrogant men of their own will
Consider this wayward poet of yours a rival still

भड़का रहे हैं आग लबे-नग़मागर से हम

भड़का रहे हैं आग लबे-नग़मागर से हम
ख़ामोश क्या रहेंगे ज़माने के डर से हम

कुछ और बढ़ गये जो अंधेरे तो क्या हुआ
मायूस तो नहीं हैं तलू-ए-सहर[1] से हम

ले-देके अपने पास फ़क़त इक नज़र तो है
क्यों देखें ज़िंदगी को किसी की नज़र से हम

माना कि इस ज़मीं को न गुलज़ार कर सके
दो ख़ार कम तो कर गये गुज़रे जिधर से हम

Bhadaka rahe hain aag labe-nagmaagar se hum
Khamosh kya rahenge zamane ke dar se hum

Kuchh aur bad gaye jo andhere to kya hua
Mayoos to nahin hain taloo-e-sahar se hum

Le-deke apne paas fakat ek nazar to hai
Kyon dekhein zindgi ko kisi ki nazar se hum

Mana ki is zameen ko na gulzaar kar sake
Do khaar kam to kar gaye guzare jidhar se hum

---

1. दिन निकलना

With songs on my lips I am lighting up a fire

With songs on my lips I am lighting up a fire
I am not the one to keep quiet because of any fear

What if the thickening darkness is coming on
We are not losing hope of a rosy dawn

All said and done, what we have is our insight
Why should we see the world with anybody else's eyes

Admitted, we could not turn this earth into a garden path
We removed a few thorns at least from wherever we passed

इस तरफ़ से गुज़रे थे क़ाफ़िले बहारों के

इस तरफ़ से गुज़रे थे क़ाफ़िले बहारों के
आज तक सुलगते हैं ज़ख्म रहगुज़ारों के

ख़िलवतों[1] *के शैदाई ख़िलवतों में खुलते हैं*
हम से पूछकर देखो राज़ परदादारों के

पहले हंस के मिलते हैं फिर नज़र चुराते हैं
आशना-सिफ़त हैं लोग अजनबी दयारों के

शग़ले-मयपरस्ती गो जश्ने नामुरादी था
यूं ही कट गये कुछ दिन तेरे सोगवारों के

Is taraf se guzare the kaafile bahaaron ke
Aaj tak sulgate hain zakhm rahguzaaron ke

Khilwata ke shaidai khilwaton mein khulte hain
Hum se poochkar dekho raj pardadaron ke

Pahle hans ke milte hain phir nazar churate hain
Aashna-sifat hain log ajnabi dayaaron ke

Shagale-mayparasti go jashne namuradi tha
Yun hi kat gaye kuchh din tere sogwaron ke.

---

1. तनहाई

The caravans of spring

The caravans of spring had once passed this way
The wounds of the pathway fester till even today

The lovers of solitude open up in solitude only
You may ask us as well the secrets of veiled reality

These strangers are quite sociable but only for a while
They side-step us now but earlier they would meet us with a smile

Our occasioned binge drinking though marked our failure
This was the way your stricken ones passed their days, however

देखा तो था यूंही किसी ग़फ़लत-शिआर ने

देखा तो था यूंही किसी ग़फ़लत-शिआर[1] ने
दीवाना कर दिया दिले-बेइख़्तियार ने
ऐ आरज़ू के धुंधले ख़्वाबो! जवाब दो
फिर किस की याद आई थी मुझको पुकारने?
तुमको ख़बर नहीं मगर इक सादालौह[2] को
बर्बाद कर दिया तेरे दो दिन के प्यार ने
मैं और तुम से तर्के-मोहब्बत की[3] आरज़ू
दीवाना कर दिया है ग़मे-रोज़गार[4] ने
अब ऐ दिले-तबाह! तेरा क्या ख़्याल है।
हम तो चले थे काकुले-गेती[5] संवारने

Dekha toh tha yunhi kisi gafalat-shiaar ne
Diwana kar diya dile-beikhtiyaar ne
E aarajoo ke dhundhle khwabon! jawab do
Phir kis ki yaad aai thi mujhko pukarne?
Tumko khabar nahi magar ek sadalauh ko
Barbaad kar diya tere do din ke pyaar ne
Main aur tum se tarke-mohabbat ki aarjoo
Diwana kar diya hai ghame-rozgaar ne
Ab e dile-tabah! tera kya khyaal hai
Hum toh chale the kakule-geti sawarne

---

1. लापरवाही जिंसका स्वभाव हो 2. सरल स्वभाव 3. प्यार करना छोड़ना 4. सांसारिक दुखों ने 5. संसार के केश

Somebody had looked at me most causually

Somebody had looked at me most causually
But my wilful heart has turned me crazy

O the hazy dreams of desire, you answer me
Whose memory crossed my mind and once again called for me

You do not know that a plain and simple person
Has been undone by your shortlived affection

How can I ever think of bidding your love good-bye
The sorrows of work-a-day life have turned me crazy

Now o ruined heart, what is your plan
I am setting out to change the fortunes of man

अहले दिल और भी हैं!

अहले-दिल[1] *और भी हैं, अहले-वफ़ा*[2] *और भी हैं*
एक हम ही नहीं, दुनिया से ख़फ़ा[3] *और भी हैं*

हम पे ही ख़त्म नहीं मस्लके-शोरीदा सरी[4]
चाक-दिल[5] *और भी हैं, चाक-कबा*[6] *और भी हैं*

क्या हुआ गर मेरे यारों की ज़बानें चुप हैं
मेरे शाहिद[7] *मेरे यारों के सिवा और भी हैं*

सर सलामत है तो क्या संगे-मलामत[8] *की कमी*
जान बाक़ी है तो पैकाने-कज़ा[9] *और भी हैं*

मुन्सिफ़े शहर[10] *की वहदत*[11] *पे न हर्फ़*[12] *आ जाए*
लोग कहते हैं कि अरबाबे-जफ़ा[13] *और भी हैं*

Ahle-dil aur bhi hain, ahle-wafa aur bhi hain
Ek hum hi nahin, duniya se khafa aur bhi hain

Hum pe hi khatm nahin maslake-shorida sari
Chak-dil aur bhi hain, chak-kabaa aur bhi hain

Kya hua gar mere yaroon ki zabaanein chup hain
Mere shaahid mere yaaron ke siwa aur bhi hain

Sar salaamat hai to kya sange-malaamat ki kami
Jaan baki hai to paikane-kaza aur bhi hain

Munsife shahar ki wahdat pe na harf aa jaye
Log kahte hain ki arbabe-jafa aur bhi hain

---

1. दिल वाले 2. वफ़ा करने वाले 3. नाराज़ 4. पागलपन का पंथ 5. जिनके दिल टूट चुके हैं 6. फटे चोले वाले 7. साक्षी, गवाह 8. दुत्कार के लिए मारा गया पत्थर 9. मौत के तीर 10. न्यायाधीश 11. निष्पक्षता 12. आंच 13. कष्ट देने वाले

There are others too with a heart

There are others too with a heart, other men of their world as well
I am not the only one angry with world, I can tell

The creed of madness doesn't end just with us
There are others too with broken hearts others too with tattered dress

If my comrades choose to be silent, let them do
I have witnesses other than these friends too

If your head is still intact, there is no dearth of accusations
If you are alive, there are other arrows for you too

Nothing should be done to impair the judge's impartiality
People say there are others too who can be a source of your misery

ख़ुद्दारियों के ख़ून को

ख़ुद्दारियों के ख़ून को अर्ज़ां[1] न कर सके
हम अपने जौहरों को नुमायां न कर सके
होकर ख़राबे-मय[2] तेरे ग़म तो भुला दिए
लेकिन ग़मे-हयात का[3] दरमां[4] न कर सके
टूटा तिलिस्मे-अहदे-मोहब्बत[5] कुछ इस तरह
फिर आरज़ू की शम्अ फ़रोज़ां न कर सके[6]
किस दर्जा दिलशिकन[7] थे मोहब्बत के हादिसे
हम ज़िंदगी में फिर कोई अरमां न कर सके
मायूसियों ने छीन लिए दिल के वलवले
वो भी निशाते-रूह का[8] सामां न कर सके

Khudariyon ke khoon ko arzaa na kar sake
Hum apne jauharon ko numayan na kar sake
Hokar kharabe-may tere gham to bhula diye
Lekin ghame-hayaat ka darmaan na kar sake
Toota tilisme-ahde-mohabbat kuchh is tarah
Phir aarzoo ki shma farozan na kar sake
Kis darja dilshik the mohabbat ke hadise
Hum zindgi main phir koi armaan na kar sake
Maayusiyon ne chhin liye dil ke valvale
Vo bhi nishaate-rooh ka saman na kar sake

---

1. सस्ता 2. शराब के हाथों तबाह होकर 3. जीवन के दुख का 4. इलाज 5. प्रेम-काल का जादू 6. हृदय-भंजक 7. आत्मा की तृप्ति या हर्ष का

My self-respect

I could not compromise my self-respect
And as a result, could not show myself at my best

By drowning myself in alcohol, I could forget the pain
that you gave me though
I could find no cure for sufferings of life even so

The spell that your love had cast was broken in such
a way
That any desire for love ever after was swept away

My tragedy in love was so heart-breaking
That after that, I had no desire for anything

Despair so much sapped my spirit
That even she could not bring any cheer

हवस-नसीब नज़र को कहीं क़रार नहीं

हवस-नसीब[1] नज़र को कहीं क़रार[2] नहीं
मैं मुन्तज़िर हूं, मगर तेरा इन्तिज़ार नहीं

हमीं से रंगे-गुलिस्तां; हमीं से रंगे-बहार
हमीं को निज़ामे-गुलिस्तां[3] पे इख़्तियार नहीं

अभी न छेड़ मोहब्बत के गीत ऐ मुतरिब[4]
अभी हयात[5] का माहौल[6] खुशगवार नहीं

तुम्हारे अहदे-वफ़ा[7] को मैं अहद क्या समझूं
मुझे खुद अपनी मोहब्बत का एतिबार नहीं

Havas-nasib nazar ko kahin karar nahin
Main muntzir hoon, magar tera intizar nahin

Hamin se range-gulistan, hamin se range-bahar
Hamin ko nizame-gulistan pe ikhtiyaar nahin

Abhi na chhed mohabbat ke geet ye mutrib
Abhi hayaat ka mahaul khushgwar nahin

Tumhare ahde-wafa ko main ahad kya samjhun
Mujhe khud apni mohabbat ka etibaar nahin

---

1. लोलुपता-प्रिय 2. चैन 3. उद्यान की व्यवस्था 4. गायक 5. जीवन 6. वातावरण 7. वफ़ादार रहने की प्रतिज्ञा

A lustful eye cannot find peace anywhere

A lustful eye cannot find peace anywhere
I am waiting but not waiting for you here

It is because of us that garden has lustre, and so has
the spring
And it is we who have been denied a say in the
garden's functioning

Sing not the songs of love just yet, o singer
The circumstances are as yet not fit for it

How can I accept your promise of love as true
I do not trust my own love too

I cannot escape life to be sure
But I do not mind death either

O Where have the times brought me now
Things, O life are now beyond you too

मोहब्बत तर्क की मैंने

मोहब्बत तर्क की मैंने, गरेबां सी लिया मैंने
ज़माने अब तो खुश हो, ज़हर ये भी पी लिया मैंने

अभी ज़िन्दा हूं लेकिन सोचता रहता हूं ख़ल्वत[1] में
कि अब तक किस तमन्ना के सहारे जी लिया मैंने

उन्हें अपना नहीं सकता, मगर इतना भी क्या कम है
कि कुछ मुद्दत हसीं ख़्वाबों में खोकर जी लिया मैंने

बस अब तो दामने-दिल छोड़ दो बेकार उम्मीदो
बहुत दुख सह लिए मैंने, बहुत दिन जी लिया मैंने

Mohabbat tark ki maine, gareban si liya maine
Zamane ab toh khush ho, zahar ye bhi pi liya maine

Abhi zinda hun lekin sochata rahata hun khalwat mein
Ki ab tak kis tamnna ke sahare ji liya maine

Unhe aapna nahi sakta magar itna bhi kya kam hai
Ki kuchh muddat hansi khawabon mein khokar ji liya maine

Bas ab toh damne-dil chhhor do bekar ummidon
Bahut dukh sah liye maine, bahut din ji liya maine

---

1. एकांत

I have said good-bye to love

I have said good-bye to love, my waywardness forsaken
O world, be happy now, this bitter pill too I have taken

I am alive still but, when alone, I keep wondering
On what hope have I been so far living

I cannot make her my own, but is it not sufficient at is seems
That at least for a few days I have lived with happy dreams

Now at least give up these vain hopes, leave it o heart
I have lived enough already I have suffered a lot

आवाज़े-आदम [1]

दबेगी कब तलक आवाज़े-आदम, हम भी देखेंगे
रुकेंगे कब तलक जज़्बाते-बरहम [2] हम भी देखेंगे
चलो यूं ही सही ये जौरे-पैहम [3] हम भी देखेंगे

दरे-ज़िंदां [4] से देखें या उरूजे-दार से [5] देखें
तुम्हें रुसवा [6] सरे-बाज़ारे-आलम [7] हम भी देखेंगे
ज़रा दम लो मआले-शौकते-जम हम भी देखेंगे

ब-ज़ोमे-कुव्वते-फ़ौलादो-आहन [8] देख लो तुम भी
ब-फ़ैज़े-जज़्बा-ए-ईमाने-मोहकम [9] हम भी देखेंगे
जबीने-कज-कुलाही [10] ख़ाक पर ख़म [11] हम भी देखेंगे

→

Dabegi kab talak aawazen-aadam, hum bhi dekhenge
Rukenge kab talak jazbaate-barham hum bhi dekhenge
Chalo yun hi sahi ye jore-paiham hum bhi dekhenge

Dare-zinda se dekhe ya urooje-daar se dekhen
Tumhe ruswa sare-bazare-aalam hum bhi dekhenge
Zara dam lo maale-shaukate-jam hum bhi dekhenge

B-zome-kuvvate-faulado-aahan dekh lo tum bhi
B-faije-jazba-e-imaane-mohkam hum bhi dekhenge
jabeene-kaj-kulaahi khaak par kham hum bhi dekhenge

---

1. मानव की आवाज़ 2. व्याकुल भावनाएं 3. लगातार अत्याचार 4. कारागार का द्वार 5. सूली के ऊपर से 6. अपमानित 7. संसार रूपी बाज़ार में 8. लोहे और फ़ौलाद (हथियारों) की शक्ति के बल पर 9. दृढ़-विश्वास की भावना की कृपा से 10. बादशाहों का माथा 11. झुका हुआ

The voice of man

How long will the voice of man be suppressed we will see
How long will his restless emotions be stifled we will see
Let there be ceaseless cruelty we will see

Whether it is from the holes in the prison or the height of the hanging place
We'll see you humbled in the world's market places
Wait a while, the end game of this Jamshed like glory, we will see

You are seeing the power of your weapons now
The power of deadly determination and your kingly arrogance rolling in dust we will see

→

मुकाफ़ाते-अ़मल[1] तारीख़े-इन्सां[2] की रवायत[3] है
करोगे कब तलक नावक[4] फ़राहम[5] हम भी देखेंगे
कहां तक है तुम्हारे ज़ुल्म में दम हम भी देखेंगे

ये हंगामे-विदा-ए-शब[6] है, ऐ ज़ुल्मत के फ़रज़न्दो[7]
सहर के दोश पर[8] गुलनार परचम[9] हम भी देखेंगे
तुम्हें भी देखना होगा ये आ़लम[10] हम भी देखेंगे

Muqafate-amal tareekhe-insaa ki rawaayat hai
Karoge kab talak naavak faraham hum bhi dekhenge
Kahan tak hai tumhare zulm mein dam hum bhi dekhenge

Ye hangame-vida-e-shab hai, ye zulmat ke farzando
Sahar ke dosh par gulnaar parcham hum bhi dekhenge
Tumhe bhi dekhna hoga ye aalam hum bhi dekhenge

---

1. क्रिया का पुनरावर्तन 2. मानव जाति का इतिहास 3. परिपाटी 4. तीर 5. एकत्रित 6. रात्रि की विदा का समय 7. अन्धकार के बेटों 8. सुबह के कन्धे पर 9. सुर्ख़ रंग का झण्डा 10. परिस्थिति

Repeating history is a part of human tradition
How long will you use the force of arms we will see
How far can you tyranny go, we will see

O sons of darkness, the times of nights' departure approaches
And aloft on the shoulders of dawn the red flag we will see.
You too will have to see the sight that we will see.

आज

साथियो! मैंने बरसों तुम्हारे लिए
चांद, तारों, बहारों के सपने बुने
हुस्न और इश्क़ के गीत गाता रहा
आरज़ुओं के ऐवां[1] सजाता रहा
मैं तुम्हारा मुग़न्नी[2], तुम्हारे लिए
जब भी आया नए गीत लाता रहा

आज लेकिन मेरे दामने-चाक में[3]
गर्दे-राहे-सफ़र के सिवा कुछ नहीं
मेरे बरबत के सीने में नग़्मों का दम घुट गया है
तानें चीख़ों के अम्बार में दब गई हैं
और गीतों के सुर हिचकियां बन गए हैं
मैं तुम्हारा मुग़न्नी हूं, नग़्मा नहीं हूं
और नग़्मे की तख़्लीक़[4] का साज़ो-सामां

→

Saathiyon! maine barason tumhare liye
Chand, taaron, baharon ke sapne bune
Husn aur ishq ke geet gata raha
Aarzuaon ke aewan sajata raha
Main tumhara mughnni, tumhare liye
Jab bhi aaya naye geet lata raha

Aaj lekin mere damane-chaak mein
Garde-raahe-safar ke siwa kuchh nahin
Mere barbat ke sine mein nagmon ka dam ghut gaya hai
Taanen chikhon ke ambaar mein dab gai hain
Aur geeton ke sur hichkiyan ban gaye hain
Main tumhara muganni hoon, nagma nahin hoon
Aur nagme ki takhleek ka sazo-saman

---

1. मनोकामनाओं के महल 2. संगीतकार 3. फटे हुए दामन में 4. रचना

Today

Comrades, for years now
I have woven for you the dreams of the moon, stars and spring
Sung the songs of love and beauty
Built palaces after your heart
And whenever I came
I brought new songs

But today I have brought with me nothing
Except the dust and grime
That has stuck to me during my journey
My songs lie suffocated inside my musical instrument
And their tunes lie buried under a heap of shrieks and cries

→

साथियो! आज तुमने भस्म कर दिया है
और मैं—अपना टूटा हुआ साज़ थामे
सर्द लाशों के अम्बार को तक रहा हूं
मेरे चारों तरफ़ मौत की वहशतें[1] नाचती हैं
और इन्सान की हैवानियत जाग उठी है
बर्बरियत[2] के ख़ूख़्वार अफ़रीत[3]
अपने नापाक जबड़ों को खोले
ख़ून पी-पी के गुर्रा रहे हैं
बच्चे माओं की गोदों में सहमे हुए हैं
इस्मतें[4] सर-बिरहना[5] परेशान हैं
हर तरफ़ शोरे-आहो-बुका[6] है
और मैं इस तबाही के तूफ़ान में
आग और ख़ून के हेजान[7] में
सरनिगूं[8] और शिकस्ता[9] मकानों के मलबे से पुर रास्तों पर

→

Sathio! aaj tumne bhasm kar diya hai
Aur main - apna toota hua saaz thame
Sard laashon ke ambaar ko tak raha hoon
Mere charon taraf maut ki vahshat nachati hain
Aur insaan ki haiwaniyat jaag uthi hai
Barbariyat ke khukhwar afreet
Apne napaak jabaron ko khole
Khoon pi-pi ke gurra rahe hain
Bachche maaon ki godon mein sahme huye hain
Ismate sar-birhana pareshan hain
Har taraf shore-aaho-buka hai
Aur main is tabahi ke tufaan mein
Aag aur khoon ke hejaan mein
Sarnigoon aur shikasta makanon ke malbe se pur raston par

---

1. वीभत्सताएं 2. बर्बरता 3. राक्षस 4. स्त्रीत्व 5. नंगे सिर 6. आहों और विलाप का शोर
7. उथल-पुथल 8. जिनका सिर झुका है (छतें टूटी हुई हैं) 9. टूटे-फूटे

And today, O comrades you have destroyed the
wherewithal of those songs.
Now holding a broken instrument in my hand
I am witnessing a heap of cold corpses,
All around me I witness a dance of death
Witness the animality of man
I see the barbaric hordes
With their jaws wide open
Drinking blood and growling
Children lie petrified in their mother's lap
Womanhood is bewildered and helpless
And all around me I hear only sighs and cries
In this whirlwind of destruction
In this havoc of blood and fire
In the midst of decimated houses

→

अपने नग़्मों की झोली पसारे
दर-ब-दर फिर रहा हूं–
मुझको अमन और तहज़ीब की भीख दो
मेरे गीतों की लय, मेरे सुर, मेरी नै
मेरे मजरूह[1] होंटों को फिर सौंप दो
साथियो! मैंने बरसों तुम्हारे लिए
इंक़िलाब और बग़ावत के नग़्मे अलापे
अजनबी[2] राज़ के ज़ुल्म की छांव में
सरफ़रोशी[3] के ख़्वाबीदा[4] जज़्बे[5] उभारे
इस सुबह की राह देखी
जिसमें इस मुल्क की रूह आज़ाद हो
आज ज़ंजीरे-महकूमियत[6] कट चुकी है
और इस मुल्क के बह्र रो-बर[7], बामो-दर[8]
अजनबी क़ौम के ज़ुल्मत-अफ़शां[9] फरेरे[10] की मनहूस
छांव से आज़ाद हैं

→

Apne nagmon ki jholi pasaare
Dar-b-dar phir raha hoon -
Mujhko aman aur tahzeeb ki bheekh do
Mere geeton ki lay, mere sur, meri nai
Mere majrooh honton ko phir saunp do
Sathio! maine barson tumhare liye
Inkilaab aur baghawat ke nagme alape
Ajnabi raj ke zulm ki chhanv mein
Sarfaroshi ke khwabeeda jazbe ubhare
Is subah ki raah dekhi
Jismein is mulk ki rooh aazad ho
Aaj janjire-mahkumiyat kat chuki hai
Aur is mulk ke bah ro-bar, bamo-dar
Ajnabi kaum ke zulmat-afashan farere ki manhoos
Chhanv se aazad hain

---

1. घायल 2. विदेशी 3. सिर बेचने (कटवाने) 4. सोए हुए 5. भावनाएं 6. दासता की बेड़ी 7. समुद्र और धरती 8. छत और द्वार 9. अन्धकार फैलाने वाले 10. झण्डे

I am moving from door to door
Displaying my songs and begging to give me peace
and civilized behaviour in alms
Begging them to give my withered lips
The voice, the rhythm and the melody of my songs
Comrades I have for years sung for you
Songs of revolution and revolt
And under the tyranny of foreign rule
Roused you for supreme sacrifice
Only to see the dawn of the day
When the spirit of this country is liberated
Today the shackles of slavery are broken
And every nook and corner of this nation
Has come out of the darkness of foreign reign

→

खेत सोना उगलने को बेचैन है
वादियां लहलहाने को बेताब हैं
कोहसारो[1] के सीने में हेजान है
संग और ख़िश्त[2] बेख़्वाबों-बेदार[3] हैं
इनकी आंखों में ता'मीर[4] के ख़्वाब हैं
इनके ख़्वाबों को तकमील[5] का रूप दो
मुल्क की वादियां, घाटियां, खेतियां, औरतें, बच्चियां–
हाथ फैलाए ख़ैरात की मुन्तज़िर[6] हैं
इनको अम्न और तहज़ीब की भीख दो
मांओं को उनके होंटों की शादाबियां[7]
नन्हे बच्चों को उनकी खुशी बख़्श दो
मुझको मेरा हुनर, मेरी लय बख़्श दो
मेरे सुर बख़्श दो, मेरी नै बख़्श दो
आज सारी फ़ज़ा[8] भिकारी है

→

Khet sona ugalne ko bechain hai
Wadiyan lahlahane ko betab hain
Kohsaaron ke sine mein hejaan hai
Sang aur khisht bekhwabon-bedar hain
Inki aankhon mein taameer ke khwab hain
Inke khwabon ko takmeel ka roop do
Mulk ki wadion, ghatiyon, khetiyon, aauratein, bachchiyan–
Hath phailaye khairat ki muntzir hain
Inko aman aur tahzeeb ki bheekh do
Maaon ko unke honton ki shadabiyan
Nanhe bachchon ko unki khushi bakhsh do
Mujhko mera hunar, meri lay bakhsh do
Mere sur bakhsh do, meri nai bakhsh do
Aaj saari faza bhikari hai

---

1. पहाड़ों 2. पत्थरों और ईंट 3. जागरूक 4. निर्माण 5. पूर्णता 6. प्रतीक्षा में 7. तरावट 8. वातावरण

Its fields are eager to burst with their golden yield
Its valleys are keen to bloom
There is stirring in mountains
Even its rock and bricks pulsate with life
In every eye there is a dream of rebirth reconstruction
Fulfil their dream,
The fields and valleys as also the women and girls of this country
Are begging for peace and civilized behavior
Grant them their wish
Give back to the mothers their smile
To the kids their innocent joys
And give back to me,
My voice, my rhyme, my rhythm, my art
Every creature is carrying a begging bowl

→

और मैं इस भिखारी फ़ज़ा में
अपने नग़्मों की झोली पसारे
दर-ब-दर फिर रहा हूं
मुझको फिर मेरा खोया हुआ साज़ दो
मैं तुम्हारा मुग़न्नी—तुम्हारे लिए
जब भी आया, नए गीत लाता रहूंगा

Aur main is bhikhari faza mein
Apne nagmon ko jholi pasaare
Dar-b-dar phir raha hoon
Mujhko phir mera khoya hua saaz do
Main tumhara mughnni–tumhare liye
Jab bhi aaya, naye geet lata rahoonga

And among them, I too am going from door to door
Begging for my musical instrument, lost
Begging back my songs
For your singer, that I am
Whenever I come
I will come with new songs for you

(Recited at All India Radio New Delhi on
11th September, 1947)

ज़िंदगी से उन्स है

ज़िंदगी से उन्स[1] है
हुस्न से लगाव है
धड़कनों में आज भी इश्क़ का अलाव है
दिल अभी बुझा नहीं

रंग भर रहा हूं मैं
ख़ाका ए-हयात[2] में
आज भी हूं मुन्हमिक[3]
फ़िक्रे-कायनात[4] में
ग़म अभी लुटा नहीं

तुम ही तज़वीज़े-सुलह[5] लाते हो
तुम ही सामाने-जंग बांटते हो
तुम ही करते हो क़त्ल का मातम
तुम ही तीरों-तफ़ंग[6] बांटते हो

Zindgi se uns hai
Husn se lagaav hai
Dhadkanon mein aaj bhi ishq ka alaav hai
Dil abhi bujha nahin

Rang bhar raha hoon main
Khaka-e-hayaat mein
Aaj bhi hoon munhamik
Phikre-kaynaat mein
Gham abhi luta nahin

Tum hi tazveeze-sulah laate ho
Tum hi samane-jang bantte ho
Tum hi karte ho qatl ka matam
Tum hi teeron-tafang bante ho

---

1. प्रेम, अनुराग 2. जीवन चित्र 3. व्यस्त 4. जग की चिन्ता 5. समझौते की योजना 6. तीर और बन्दूक अर्थात् जंग का सामान

I love life

I love life
I am an admirer of beauty
My heart is still alive
And the fires of love warm my heartbeats even today

I am lending colour to the blank pages of life
I am concerned even today about the state of the universe
And still have a feeling heart

It is you who bring proposals of peace
It is you who mourn over assassination
And, and
It is you who distribute deadly weapons

दो क़ते

न मुंह छुपा के जिये हम न सर झुका के जिये
सितमगरों की नज़र से नज़र मिला के जिये
अब एक रात जो कम जिये तो कम ही सही
यही बहुत है कि हम मशअलें जला के जिए

वजह-बेरगिए-गुलज़ार[1] कहूं तो क्या कहूं
कौन है कितना गुनहगार कहूं कि न कहूं
तुम जो बात सरे-बज़्म न सुनना चाहो
मैं वही बात सरे-दार[2] कहूं कि न कहूं

Na munh chhupa ke jiye hum na sar jhuka ke jiye
Sitamgaron ki nazar se nazar mila ke jiye
Ab ek raat jo kam jiye to kam hi sahi
Yahi bahut hai ki hum mashalyein jalaa ke jiye

Wajah-bergiye-gulzaar kahun to kya kahun
Kaun hai kitna gunahgaar kahun ki na kahun
Tum jo baat sare-bazm na sunna chaho
Main wahi baat sare-daar kahun ki na kahun

---

1. बाग़ उजड़ने का कारण 2. फांसी के तख़्ते पर

Two Qatas

I neither hid my face nor bowed my head in life
I saw the tyrant straight in the eye upright
It matters not if I lived one night less
But as long as I lived I lit the candle bright

What do you think would happen if I were to tell why
is the garden so lustreless
And who is and how much responsible for it
Do you know what would happen if at the gallows I
were to reveal
That which to hear in public you would unbearable
feel

किसी को उदास देखकर

तुम्हें उदास-सी पाता हूं मैं कई दिन से
न जाने कौन-से सदमे उठा रही हो तुम
वो शोख़ियां, वो तबस्सुम, वो क़हक़हे न रहे
हर एक चीज़ को हसरत से देखती हो तुम
छुपा-छुपा के ख़ामोशी में अपनी बेचैनी
ख़ुद अपने राज़ की तशहीर[1] बन गई हो तुम

मेरी उमीद अगर मिट गई तो मिटने दो
उमीद क्या है बस इक पेशो-पस[2] है कुछ भी नहीं
मेरी हयात की ग़मगीनियों का ग़म न करो
ग़मे-हयात[3] ग़मे-यक-नफ़स[4] है कुछ भी नहीं
तुम अपने हुस्न की रा'नाइयों पे[5] रहम करो
वफ़ा फ़रेब है, तूले हवस[6] है कुछ भी नहीं

→

Tumhein udaas-si pata hoon main kai din se
Na jane kaun-se sadme utha rahi ho tum
Wo shokhiyan, wo tabssum, wo kahkahe na rahe
Har ek cheez ko hasrat se dekhti ho tum
Chhupa-chhupa ke khamoshi mein apni bechaini

Meri umeed agar mit gai to mitne do
umeed kya hai bas ek pesho-pas hai kuchh bhi nahin
Mere hayaat ki ghamginiyon ka gham na karo
Ghame-hayaat gham-yak-nafas hai kuchh bhi nahin
Tum apne husn ki ranaiyon pe raham karo
Wafa fareb hai, tule hawas hai kuchh bhi nahin

---

1. विज्ञापन 2. दुविधा 3. जीवन का ग़म 4. क्षण-भर का ग़म (एक श्वास से सम्बन्धित)
5. रमणीयताओं पर 6. लोलुपता का विस्तार

On seeing somebody sad

I have found you sad for some days now
God knows what calamities have befallen you
That charm, that smile, those peals of laughter
Have all disappeared
And you look at everything with a wistful eye
And by your restlessness, you reveal it all the more

Let my hopes be dashed
Hope is nothing but your 'yes' and `no' alternating
Don't be saddened by my sorrow
Hope is transient like a passing breath
You should take care of your charm and beauty
Fidelity is only a deception, a euphemism for lust

→

मुझे तुम्हारे तग़ाफ़ुल[1] से क्यों शिकायत हो
मेरी फ़ना[2] मेरे एहसास का[3] तक़ाज़ा है
मैं जानता हूं कि दुनिया का ख़ौफ़ है तुमको
मुझे ख़बर है, ये दुनिया अजीब दुनिया है
यहां हयात के पर्दे में मौत पलती है
शिकस्ते-साज़ की[4] आवाज़ रूहे-नग़्मा है

मुझे तुम्हारी जुदाई का कोई रंज नहीं
मेरे ख़याल की दुनिया में मेरे पास हो तुम
ये तुमने ठीक कहा है, तुम्हें मिला न करूं
मगर मुझे ये बता दो कि क्यों उदास हो तुम
ख़फ़ा न होना मेरी जुर्रते-तख़ातब पर[5]
तुम्हें ख़बर है मेरी ज़िंदगी की आस हो तुम

मेरा तो कुछ भी नहीं है मैं रो के जी लूंगा
मगर ख़ुदा के लिए तुम असीरे-ग़म[6] न रहो
हुआ ही क्या जो ज़माने ने तुमको छीन लिया

→

Mujhe tumhare tagaaful se kyon shikayat ho
Meri fanaa mere aehsaas ka taqaja hai
Main janta hoon ki duniya ka kauf hai tumko
Mujhe khaba hai, ye duniya ajeeb duniya hai
Yahan hayaat ke parde mein maut palti hai
Shikste-saaz ki aawaz roohe-nagma hai

Mujhe tumhari judai ka koi ranj nahin
Mere khyaal ki duniya mein mere paas ho tum
Ye tumne thik kaha hai, tumhein mila na karoon
Magar mujhe ye bataa do ki kyon udaas ho tum
Khafaa na hona mere jurute-takhaatab par

Mera to kuchh bhi nahin hai main ro ke ji loonga
Magar khuda ke liye tum asire-gham na raho
Hua hi kya jo zamaane ne tumko chhin liya

---

1. उपेक्षा 2. नाश 3. चेतना का 4. साज़ के टूटने की 5. सम्बोधन के दुःसाहस पर 6. शोक-ग्रस्त

Why should I mind your indifference
My ruin inheres in my sensitiveness
I know you are afraid of the world
And the world is quite a strange place
Death appears here in the form of life, I know
And the broken musical instruments produce the sweetest music

I am not troubled by your parting from me
For, you are always with me in my imagination
You are right in asking me not to meet you, but please tell me why you are so sad
Don't mind my audacity to say
That you are the only hope of my life

Bother not for me, I can live this life in tears
But for heaven's sake, don't be stricken with grief
What if the world has snatched you from me

→

यहां पे कौन हुआ है किसी का, सोचो तो
मुझे क़सम है मेरी दुख-भरी जवानी की
मैं खुश हूं मेरी मोहब्बत के फूल ठुकरा दो

मैं अपनी रूह की हर इक ख़ुशी मिटा लूंगा
मगर तुम्हारी मसर्रत मिटा नहीं सकता
मैं खुद को मौत के हाथों में सौंप सकता हूं
मगर ये बारे-मसाइब[1] उठा नहीं सकता
तुम्हारे ग़म के सिवा और भी तो ग़म हैं मुझे
नजात जिनसे मैं इक लमहा[2] पा नहीं सकता

ये ऊंचे-ऊंचे मकानों की ड्योढ़ियों के तले
हर एक गाम पे[3] भूके भिकारियों की सदा[4]
हर एक घर में ये इफ़्लास और भूक का शोर
हर एक सम्त[5] ये इन्सानियत की आहो-बुका[6]

→

Yahan pe kaun hua hai kisi ka, socho to
Mujhe kasam hai meri dhukh-bhari jawani ki
Main khush hoon mere mohabbat ke phool thukra do

Main apni rooh ki har ek khushi mita loonga
Magar tumhari masrrat mita nahin sakta
Main khud ko maut ke hathon mein saunp sakta hoon
Magar ye baare-massaib utha nahin sakta
Tumhare gham ke siwa aur bhi to gham hain mujhe
Najaat jinse main ek lamha pa nahin sakta

Ye unche-unche makano ki dyodhiyon ke tale
Har ek gaam pe bhooke bhikariyon ki sadaa
Ha ek ghar mein ye iflaas aur bhook ka shor
Har ek samt ye insaaniyat ki aaho-buka

---

1. मुसीबतों का बोझ 2. क्षण-भर के लिए 3. क़दम पर 4. आवाज़ 5. ओर 6. आहों का शोर

No one can claim anybody for his own
I swear by my miserable youth,
I don't mind that you turn down my offer of love

I will wipe out all joy from my heart
But cannot see your happiness turning into sorrow
I can hand myself over to death
But cannot bear the burden of your being in misery
Apart from sorrowing for you
I have other sorrows too
From which even for a moment there is no relief

In the backdrop of tall mansions here
I hear the starving beggars calling
Hunger and poverty stalking everywhere
I hear the hammer falling and beating

→

ये कारख़ानों में लोहे का शोरो-गुल जिसमें
है दफ़्न लाखों ग़रीबों की रूह का नग़्मा

ये शाहराहों पे[1] रंगीन साड़ियों की झलक
ये झोंपड़ों में ग़रीबों के बेकफ़न लाशें
ये माल रोड पे कारों की रेल-पेल का शोर
ये पटरियों पे ग़रीबों के ज़र्द-रू[2] बच्चे

गली-गली में ये बिकते हुए जवां चेहरे
हसीन आंखों में अफ़सुर्दगी-सी[3] छाई हुई
ये जंग और ये मेरे वतन के शोख़ जवां
ख़रीदी जाती हैं उठती जवानियां जिनकी
ये बात-बात पे क़ानूनो-ज़ाब्ते की गिरफ़्त[4]
ये ज़िल्लतें, ये ग़ुलामी, ये दौरे-मजबूरी
ये ग़म बहुत हैं मेरी ज़िंदगी मिटाने को
उदास रहके मेरे दिल को और रंज न दो

Ye kaarkhanon mein lohe ka shoro-gul jismein
Hain dafn laakhon garibon ki rooh ka nagma

Ye shaahrahon pe rangeen saariyon ki jhalak
Ye jhopdon mein garibon ke bekafan laashein
Ye maal rod pe kaaron ki rel-pel ka shor
Ye patriyon pe garibon ke zard-roo bachchein

Gali-gali mein ye bikte huye jawaan chehre
Haseen aankhon mein afarsudgi-si chhai hui
Ye jang aur ye mere vatan ke shokh jawaan
Kharidi jati hain uthati jawaniyan jinki
Ye baat-baat pe kanoono-zabte ki girft
Ye zillatein, ye ghulaami, ye daure-majboori
Ye gham bahut hain meri zindgi mitane ko
Udaas rahke mere dil ko aur ranj na do

---

1. राजपथों पर 2. पीले चेहरे वाले 3. उदासी-सी 4. पकड़

The iron into shape in the factories everywhere
Burying the joys of millions underneath its noise

I see an array of shining sarees on the highway
As also the pale faces of the children in the hutments
Of the poor
I see cars zooming past on the Mall Road
As also the pale faces of children of the poor on the
pavements

These youthful maidens for sale in every street
The lovely eyes filled with despair,
I see the strapping young men of my country selling
themselves for the war
I see the heavy hand of law in action everywhere
Their humiliation, helplessness and slavery—

These sorrows are enough to finish my life
By your sadness add not to my suffering, and strife

मेरे गीत तुम्हारे हैं

अब तक मेरे गीतों में उम्मीद भी थी पसपाई भी
मौत के क़दमों की आहट भी, जीवन की अंगड़ाई भी
मुस्तक़बिल [1] की किरनें भी थीं, हाल की बोझिल ज़ुल्मत [2] भी
तूफ़ानों का शोर भी था और ख़्वाबों की शहनाई भी

आज से मैं अपने गीतों में आतश-पारे [3] भर दूंगा
मद्धम लचकीली तानों में जीवन-धारे भर दूंगा
जीवन के अंधियारे पथ पर मशअ़ल लेकर निकलूंगा
धरती के फैले आंचल में सुर्ख़ सितारे भर दूंगा

आज से ऐ मज़दूर-किसानो! मेरे राग तुम्हारे हैं
फ़ाक़ाकश इन्सानो! मेरे जोग बिहाग तुम्हारे हैं
जब तक तुम भूखे-नंगे हो, ये शोले ख़ामोश न होंगे
जब तक बे-आराम हो तुम, ये नग़्मे राहतकश [4] न होंगे
→

Ab tak mere geeton mein ummeed bhi thi paspaai bhi
Maut ke kadamon ki aahat bhi, jiwan ki angdaai bhi
Mustkabil ki kiranein bhi thin, haal ko bojhil zulmat bhi
Tofaanon ka shor bhi tha aur khwabon ki shahnaai bhi

Aaj se main apne geeton mein aatsh-paare bhar doonga
Maddham lachkili taanon mein jiwan-dhare bhar doonga
Jiwan ke anchiyaare path par mashaal lekar nikloonga
Dharti ke phaile aanchal mein surkh sitaare bhar doonga

Aaj se ye mazdoor-kisano! mere raag tumhare hain
faakaakash insaano! mere jog bihaag tumhare hain
Jab tak tum bhookhe-nange ho, ye shole khamosh na honge
Jab tak be-aaram ho tum, ye nagme raahatkash na honge

---

1. भविष्य 2. अंधकार 3. अग्नि-पुंज 4. आनन्ददायक

My songs belong to you

Till now, my songs had both hope and despair
They echoed the advancing steps of death and showed
a rising tide of life as well
They reflected both the bright future and heavy gloom
of the past

But from today I'll fill these songs with fire
In place of the soft and swinging tunes there will be a
note of audacity and courage
On the dark pathways of life, I will go with a blazing
light
And strew red stars over the vast stretch of the earth

You peasants and workers, from today, my songs
belong to you
You starving masses, all your joys and sorrows will be
mine too
As long as you are unclad and hungry, these flames
will not go cold
Until you are at ease, my songs will provide no comfort

→

मुझको इसका रंज नहीं है लोग मुझे फ़नकार न मानें
फ़िक्रो-सुख़न के ताजिर मेरे शे'रों को अशआ़र न मानें
मेरा फ़न, मेरी उम्मीदें, आज से तुमको अर्पन हैं
आज से मेरे गीत तुम्हारे दुख और सुख का दर्पन हैं

तुम से कुव्वत[1] लेकर अब मैं तुमको राह दिखाऊंगा
तुम परचम[2] लहराना साथी, मैं बरबत पर गाऊंगा
आज से मेरे फ़न का मक़सद[3] ज़ंजीरें पिघलाना है
आज से मैं शबनम के बदले अंगारे बरसाऊंगा

Mujhko iska ranj nahin hai log mujhe fankaar na manein
Fikro-sukhan ke taajir mere shero ko ashaar na manein
Mera fan, meri ummeedein, aaj se tumko arpan hain
Aaj se mere geet tumhare dhuk aur sukh ka darpan hain

Tum se quvvat lekar ab main tumko raah dikhaoonga
Tum parcham lahrana saathi, main barbat par gaaoonga
Aaj se mere fan ka maqsad zanjeerein pighlana hai
Aaj se main shabnam ke badle angaare barsaaoonga

---

1. शक्ति 2. पताका 3. उद्देश्य

I don't mind if people don't consider me as an artist from today
Those who trade in poetry, do not accept me as a poet
From today I dedicate my art and my future entirely to you
From today, my songs will mirror only your troubles and triumphs

Taking strength from you I will now show you the way-
You carry the flag, I will sing on the lyre
The purpose of my. art from today is to melt the chains
And I will ensure that instead of dew-drops
Now from my songs only fire rains

इन्तिज़ार

चांद मद्धम है आस्मां चुप है
नींद की गोद में जहां चुप है

दूर वादी में दूधिया बादल
झुक के परबत को प्यार करते हैं
दिल में नाकाम हसरतें लेकर
हम तेरा इन्तिज़ार करते हैं

इन बहारों के साए में आ जा
फिर मोहब्बत जवां रहे न रहे
ज़िंदगी तेरे नामुरादों पर
कल तलक मेहरबां रहे न रहे

→

Chand maddham aasman chup hai
Neend ki god mein jahan chup hai

Door wadi mein dudhiya baadal
Jhuk ke parbat ko pyaar karte hain
Dil mein nakaam hasratein lekar
Hum tera intizaar karte hain

In baharon ke saaye mein aa ja
Phir mohabbat jahan rahe na rahe
Zindgi tere namuradon par
Kal talak mehrbaan rahe na rahe

Wait

The moon is dim, the sky is quiet
The world wrapped in slumber lies

The brownish clouds in a distant valley
Kiss the mountains high
Even as burning with desire
Here I wait for you

Come, it is the time of spring
Come before my love is no longer young,
Come, before life withdraws its favour
From your love-lorn ones

→

रोज़ की तरह आज भी तारे
सुबह की गर्द में न खो जाएं
आ तेरे ग़म में जागती आंखें
कम-से-कम एक रात सो जाएं

चांद मद्धम है आस्मां चुप है
नींद की गोद में जहां चुप है

Roz ki tarah aaj bhi taare
Subha ki gard mein na kho jaayein
Aa tere gham mein jaagati aankhein
Kam-se-kam ek raat so jaayein

Chand maddham hai aasman chup hai
Neend ki god mein jahan chup hai

Come before, like everyday else
The stars get lost in the morning mist
Come, so that the eyes keeping awake for your sake
Sleep at least tonight

The moon is dim, the sky is quiet
The world wrapped in slumber lies

❑❑❑

Books by Kuldip Salil

A Treasury of Urdu Poetry

A Treasury of Urdu Poetry is a treasure-house of the best of Urdu poetry from the times of the great classic poet Mir to modern day poets such as Faiz and Faraz. It contains selected ghazals and nazms of thirty-four eminent Urdu poets. Care has been taken to select only those pieces which meet the twin tests of excellence and popularity. Lovers of Urdu poetry would find this book a dream come true and a handy volume that opens a window on the world of Urdu poetry. Translation of poetry from one language to the other is extremely difficult, some would say, impossible. The challenge here is the challenge of being faithful to the original and at the same time retaining its charm and beauty. It is not only the idea of the original that is to be conveyed but its soul, its strength, its poignancy and sweetness, and if possible, its rhythm and resonance should also reach the reader.

ISBN: 9788170286911
Pages: 320

Available at all leading Bookstores or
order online from
www.rajpalpublishing.com

Books by Kuldip Salil

Diwan-e-Ghalib

With Meer, Ghalib, Iqbal and Faiz, to name only four, the firmament of Urdu poetry is truly star-studded, with numerous starlets strewn around. Ghalib has not only a pride of place among them; his stature is growing with every passing decade. He got less than his due in his own time. He was ahead of his age, and his contemporaries failed to comprehend him fully. But it was really when India (and Pakistan) celebrated his first death centenary in 1969 that he was rehabilitated as a great poet that he is. There has been no looking back after that. As with other great poets like Shakespeare, one discovers a new wealth of meaning every time one reads him, and different people find different meaning, suiting their need and situation. In other words, great poets are inexhaustible in their appeal and meaning and do not get dated even when they mirror their times most effectively. Ghalib's writings are not only an authentic account of his own age, his poetry transcends his times and situation. It is universal in its appeal.

ISBN: 9788170286929
Pages: 140

Available at all leading Bookstores or
order online from
www.rajpalpublishing.com

Books by Kuldip Salil

Best of Faraz

Ahmed Faraz is considered one of the greatest modern Urdu poets. This book offers a selection of the best ghazals of Faraz Ahmed Faraz, translated into English by Kuldip Salil. And to help you enjoy the richness and flavor of Urdu language, the original Urdu ghazals are transliterated and presented both in Roman and Devnagri script.

ISBN: 9788170289043 Pages:168

Best of Iqbal

Mohammad Iqbal was a poet and political philosopher, who is known both for his poetry and his ideas that were influential in the creation of Pakistan.This book presents a collection of some of the best poems and ghazals of Iqbal, along with their English translation as well as transliteration so that the readers can enjoy the original flavour of Urdu poetry.

ISBN: 9788170289227 Pages: 244

Books by Kuldip Salil

Best of Faiz

Faiz Ahmed Faiz is an important Urdu poet of the twentieth century who appeals to both the common man as well as the elite connoisseurs of poetry. This book offers a selection of the best of Faiz's ghazals and poems along with their English translations as well as transliterations in Roman and Devnagri Script.

ISBN: 9788170287919 Pages:176

Best of Meer

Meer Taqi Meer, the 18th century Urdu poet, is called the imam(leader) of Urdu poetry. He was highly regarded by his contemporaries and even the later poets including Ghalib who acknowledged Meer's poetic genius. Meer belonged to the Delhi school of Urdu ghazals. The greatest strength of his poetry is its simplicity. This book offers the best of Meer's ghazals along with their English translations and transliterations.

ISBN: 9788170289609 Pages:168

Available at all leading Bookstores or
order online from
www.rajpalpublishing.com